The Character
of Organizations

The Character of Organizations

Using Jungian Type in Organizational Development

William Bridges

Davies-Black Publishing
Palo Alto, Califomia

Published by Davies-Black Publishing, an imprint of Consulting Psychologists Press, Inc., 3803 East Bayshore Road, Palo Alto, CA 94303; 800-624-1765

Davies-Black and colophon are registered trademarks of Consulting Psychologists Press, Inc.

Special discounts on bulk quantities of Davies-Black Publishing books are available to corporations, professional associations, and other organizations. For details, contact the Director of Book Sales at Davies-Black Publishing, 3803 East Bayshore Road, Palo Alto, California 94303; 650-691-9123; Fax 650-988-0673.

The author would like to thank the following for permission to quote from copyrighted works. Page 13: From *Managing on the Edge* (p. 258) by R. T. Pascale, 1990, New York: Simon & Schuster. Copyright 1990 by Richard Tanner Pascale. Reprinted by permission. Page 87: From *Odyssey: From Pepsico to Apple* (p. 128) by J. Sculley, 1987, New York: HarperCollins. Copyright 1987 by HarperCollins Publishers. Reprinted by permission.

Cover illustration © Javier Romero/The Image Bank

02 01 00 99   21 20 19 18 17 16 15 14 13

Printed in the United States of America

Library of Congress Cataloging-in-Publication Data

Bridges, William

      The character of organizations : using Jungian type in organizational
  development / William Bridges
         p.   cm.
      Includes bibliographical references and index.
      ISBN 0-89106-052-9 (softcover)
      1. Organizational change. 2. Organizational behavior. 3. Corporate culture.
  I. Title.
    HD58.5.B73 1992
302.3'5—dc20

First printing 1992

91-42122
CIP

Contents

Preface

The idea of organizational character grew out of my work as a consultant to organizations in transition. I recognized very early that organizations differed in how they dealt with change. Some companies saw change coming, and others always seemed to be caught unprepared. Some organizations took big changes in stride, while others were undone by even minor ones. Some organizations were sensitive to what change did to their people; others simply announced changes and fired those who couldn't adjust.

Then, I began to look for ways to measure and describe these differences. At that time, I was using the *Myers-Briggs Type Indicator®* to help individuals distressed and dislocated by organizational change to find new career paths for themselves. As I learned more about the Jungian theories on which the MBTI® was based, I found myself thinking how often the organizations themselves behaved like individuals. I began experimenting with ways to assess an organization's "type" the way the MBTI assesses the individual's, and the result was the *Organizational Character Index* (OCI), found in Appendix A of this book.

For the past two years, I have been teaching people to work with the Index and the ideas on which it is based. I owe much that I know to the people who went through these seminars—people who challenged me to be clearer and who suggested better ways to explain an organization's characteristics. Some of those most helpful were Gail Schofield, Dick Frederickson, Ruth Morton, Tom Ucko, Tom Flautt, Dan Safran, and my daughter and associate, Margaret Bridges.

Others who helped me include Allen Hammer, my editor at Consulting Psychologists Press, whose advice was most helpful and encouraging in the task of turning concepts into text. My friend and personal editor, John Levy, also discussed my ideas, critiqued early drafts, and reviewed this manuscript. I want to thank both of them and to give special thanks to my wife, Mondi, whose understanding of Jung is much greater than mine and whose encouragement undergirds most of what I've accomplished in my life.

I can't close without a warning—and a request. The techniques for identifying organizational character and the typological categories into which the characters fall are still evolving. Since they are enormously subtle and complex, they may well *always* be evolving. Bear that in mind as you read this book and as you begin to experiment with the *Organizational Character Index*. The Index and the sixteen descriptions are not stone tablets from the mountain top. They are constantly improving and are increasingly useful mirrors or lenses with which to view organizations, but they are not perfect. You can contribute to their improvement by sharing your ideas about and experience with them. I would welcome your comments.

Chapter One

Organizational Character and Where It Comes From

The Concept of Character

Everyone knows that organizations differ in their size, structure, and purpose, but they also differ in *character*. A play-it-safe, old-line manufacturing company has a very different character from a new start-up software company. They differ in the same way that two individuals do. And the character of both the manufacturing company and the software company differ from those of a state university, a community hospital, or an architectural firm.

An organization's character is like the grain in a piece of wood. There is no such thing as good or bad grain, but some kinds of grain can take great pressure, other kinds can withstand bending or shearing forces, and still others are lovely and take a fine polish. Some are too soft or hard, too light or heavy for a particular purpose, but each has some purpose for which it is well fitted.

There are other metaphors: Character is the typical climate of the organizational country; it is the personality of the individual organization; or it is the DNA of the organizational life form. It is the organization's character that makes it feel and act like itself.

Organizational character varies greatly and subtly. In one sense, there are as many characters as there are organizations. But those infinitely varied differences can be profitably grouped into sixteen basic categories.[1] This system parallels the sixteen basic personality types as originally presented by the great Swiss psychologist, Carl Jung, and further developed by two American women, Katharine Cook Briggs and Isabel Briggs Myers. This mother–daughter team created the *Myers-Briggs Type Indicator*, or MBTI, to identify an individual's type.

As with personality type, organizational character can be established with a fair degree of objectivity. The *Organizational Character Index* , or OCI, which appears in Appendix A, does for organizations what Briggs and Myers did for individuals, although as a new instrument it has not yet been statistically validated. The OCI is still an experimental tool meant to be used by people who work with and in organizations—people who are looking for useful tools and willing to test and improve them as they use them.

The OCI is not an adaptation of the MBTI, but it is based on the same four pairs of opposing tendencies that Myers and Briggs adapted from Carl Jung's work. As adapted from the individual realm to the organizational, those scales are the following:

- *Extraversion or introversion*—the organization's orientation, the location of its reality, and the source of its energy. Is the organization primarily outwardly oriented toward markets, competition, and regulations [*extraverted*], or is it inwardly oriented toward its own technology, its leaders' dreams, or its own culture [*introverted*]?[2]

- *Sensing or intuition*—how it gathers information, what it pays attention to, how it "perceives." Is the organization primarily focused on the present, the details, and the actuality of situations [*sensing*]or on the future, the big picture, and the possibilities inherent in situations [*intuition*]?

- *Thinking or feeling*—its way of processing information, its manner of judging situations, its way of making decisions. Does the organization do these things by an impersonal process so that decision making happens on the basis of principles like consistency, competence, and efficiency [*thinking*], or through a personal process that depends on values like individuality, the common good, or creativity [*feeling*]?

- *Judging or perceiving*—does the organization tend to deal with its external world through one of the judging functions (thinking or feeling) or through one of the perceiving functions (sensing or intuition)? Organizations in which *judging* predominates prefer to reach firm decisions, define things clearly, and get closure on issues. Organizations in which *perceiving* predominates are always seeking more input, preferring to leave things loose, or opting to keep their choices open.

As with individual type, differences in organizational character shape the way in which the world is experienced. To an organization of a certain character, the world is a mass of detail, and dealing successfully with it means having everything in its place and being error-free. To an organization of a different character, the world is a vast design of great forces, and dealing successfully with it means picking up early warning signs when those forces begin to shift.

The idea that an organization has a definable character is based on an analogy: Organizations are like individuals. Like any analogy, this one must not be pushed too far. Individuals are biological creatures, while organizations are social creations. Individuals have a finite life expectancy and a biologically based life cycle, while organizations do not—they may die a natural death at the age of fifteen, or they may still be going strong at two hundred. Organizations divide, combine, grow, and shrink. There are no meaningful individual equivalents to words like divestiture, acquisition, new leadership, expansion, and downsizing.

Nonetheless, as long as it is used critically, the analogy between the organization and the individual permits us to understand and discuss certain things about organizations that would otherwise remain obscure and difficult to articulate. Specifically, it enables us to understand why organizations act as they do and why they are so very hard to change in any fundamental way. It also suggests how anyone concerned with maximizing an organization's effectiveness should go about that task.

Two Contrasting Corporate Characters: An Example

Take two companies like UPS and Federal Express. Both are in the same basic business—the shipping of packages. UPS, nicknamed "Big Brown," is an 82-year-old company that calls itself "the tightest ship in the shipping business." In a recent article, *Business Week* described UPS's internal processes in the following way:

> Endless time-and-motion studies dictate how fast delivery people should walk (three feet a second), which finger should be used to hold their keys (the middle), and how they should fold their money (face up, sequentially ordered). Packages are arranged just so in trucks equipped with skylights so that drivers can better see the labels. "They do it like clockwork," boasts strategic planner Gene Hughes. "Nothing deviates."[3]

UPS has policies and procedures to define the best way to do everything. If it were a person, we'd say that it looks at the world the way a sensing person does, focusing on the actualities of the world, not the possibilities. UPS concerns itself with a situation's details, not with the larger, but inevitably more general, picture.

UPS also functions like a thinking type person, since it calculates everything rationally without much concern for individual values or interpersonal relationships. With its penchant for defining everything completely and making a policy for every situation, it is also a judging organization.

UPS is a company that has always taken most of its cues from within, making it introverted. Again, let *Business Week*'s words make the point:

> UPS's inward focus is legendary. Founder James Casey, whose hallowed image is preserved in a near-life-size oil painting in the executive offices, set the stage in 1907 by mandating that UPS should be owned by employees

Business Week continues to describe how UPS employees typically stay with the company for a lifetime, "counting every cent as if it were their own." Even the UPS executive suite, office of Oz Nelson, who joined the company in 1959 as a salesman and is now chairman and shares a secretary with three other executives, has indoor-outdoor carpeting for flooring rather than linoleum because it is "cheaper to maintain." The point is clearly made that this kind of inward focus has caused problems.

> Concentrating on itself more than its customers has meant that UPS service has been as spartan as Nelson's office suite. UPS will cart a package nearly anywhere in the US for as little as $2.28. But don't ask the company to track it. And don't look for volume discounts.

UPS has an introverted–sensing–thinking–judging character, or as they say in the world of psychological type, it is an ISTJ organization.[4]

Federal Express is also a very successful company, but the premise behind it is different. Its founder, Frederick Smith, looked outward toward the world of customers—toward people who send packages. What do they want? he asked himself. Their world had sped up enormously since the days when UPS first grew large and powerful. Their needs had changed, and now they wanted overnight delivery, he decided. He founded a company that faced outward, toward the needs of the customer—an extraverted company.

There is another difference. Smith's company is based on an imaginative idea: People will pay for something that doesn't yet exist, something that they may not even be aware that they want. He generated the idea for

Federal Express before he had any direct experience in business, when he was a college student writing a paper for a business course. Smith's professor, who was probably less intuitive than his student, gave Smith a "C" and wasn't very impressed. But, like any good intuitive–thinking type, Smith discounted the professor's reaction—obviously the man lacked intelligence. And he went to work to invent an organization based on his creative idea about the market.

Smith was no vague dreamer. He was good at hammering out procedures and policies. His may not be "the tightest ship in the shipping business," but a company that runs its own fleet of planes and has to fit into the extremely complex schedules of the world's airports cannot be casual about details. So his òrganization, like UPS, has a bias toward judging.

Federal Express has an extraverted–intuitive–thinking–judging approach to business—which makes it an ENTJ organization. It is no accident that people have noted that Smith (a former Marine) has instilled a "bootcamp" mentality in his training programs, since one of the foremost experts on psychological type, David Keirsey, calls ENTJ people "field marshalls."

Character Differences Within a Large Organization

Similar differences usually exist within a single company or institution, not just between one of them and another. In even tightly integrated organizations, marketing and accounting have different characters. Marketing is, by definition, extraverted. Its reality is "out there" among customers and competitors, and when it wants to determine a course of action it turns outward toward them for its data. Accounting, on the other hand, looks to its own systematic processes and at the inner workings of the the organization. It is, by nature, more introverted.[5] Throughout this book, the word *organization* will be applied to both the larger entity and to the subdivisions within it. In the former category, it refers to corporations, professional firms, educational institutions, religious congregations, government agencies, nonprofit associations, and foundations.[6] In the latter category, it refers to the subdivisions of those entities that have a defined purpose and a decision-making capacity. It refers not just to the hospital but also to its billing department or laboratory, and not just to the electronics company but to its consumer products division and western region.[7]

In fact, it is generally *within* the organization—in its departments and subdivisions—that organizational character is often most reliably assessed and most useful as a concept. This is the level at which most employees either do or don't feel comfortable, where most conflicts take place between one unit and another or between one unit and the leadership of the organization as a whole. It is where missions get defined or misdefined. In short, this is where character is both most pronounced and easiest to work with. So when it comes time to determine the character of some particular organization, don't stop with establishing it for the organization as a whole. Go on and do it for the particular part of the organization—the functional, operational, or geographical unit—that most concerns you.

It is the character of each of these organizational subdivisions that one encounters when one deals with an organization. And just as type conflict can undermine and even destroy a personal relationship, it is a conflict between the dissimilar characters of two different organizations that leads to breakdowns in communication and collaboration.[7]

The character of some particular department can also vary with the customer group it serves or the setting in which it works. The nursing department of a hospital is a service function, and its service is generally quite personal. Nursing has a mission in which decisions must take feeling into account. That tendency is likely to be most pronounced in a pediatric department and least pronounced in an operating room, where technical procedures, not interpersonal relations, are what define a job well done and where thinking is an essential key function.

An elementary school is likely to be much more feeling oriented than a college, where thinking is more strongly emphasized. Teachers and administrators often reveal a similar split, with the former talking about human values (hence, feeling), while the latter talk about principles or policies (hence, thinking). Of course, the college teacher who flunks a student will probably be talking principles or policies, while the dean's office that asks that he or she be given another chance is talking about human values and approaching the case from a feeling perspective. So organizational character is somewhat situation-specific.

Where Does Character Come From?

As the examples of UPS and Federal Express have already suggested, the organization's character is originally set in large part by its founder. "An institution is the lengthened shadow of one man," said Ralph Waldo Emerson.[8]

In many organizations, the line of business, the industry, or the profession has a character of its own and is a clear influence. Military, religious, or educational work has a characterological influence. So do finance, manufacturing, entertainment, engineering, and the social services.[9] Sometimes the dominance of one or two functions in the organizational history can shape the character of the whole company—as finance has done at ISTJ General Motors or technological research has done at INTJ Digital Equipment Corporation.

There is also the generic, but very deep, influence of *business* itself and the STJ character that is businesslike. This is especially true in an age where hospitals, architectural firms, dentists' offices, think tanks, and a hundred other distinctive vocational settings are trying to do things in a more businesslike fashion. As a result, some of their professional character may be submerged by their business emphasis. So it is that a health care corporation like the Hospital Corporation of America is ESTJ, even though the field of health care is far more feeling oriented. ISTJ and ESTJ are, in fact, the most common organizational characters among American corporations.

The employee group also contributes to an organization's character, although whether that is because the particular business or profession colors the collective character of the employees, or whether it is because employees of a certain type contribute to the collective character, is hard to say. What is clear, however, is that not all engineering departments are the same—even if they are composed of people with the same personality type. Design engineers, for example, develop a more intuitive collective character than production engineers, who are more sensing. Anyone who has tried to get two such groups to collaborate on a new product know that it is like working with two siblings who don't see the world the same way and who are all the more competitive because of their other similarities.

The final source of an organization's character is its subsequent leaders. In a young organization, the founder still runs the show, so this factor does not yet exist. But with the passage of time, successive leaders, especially strong ones, put their mark on the organization. There is no doubt, for example, that much of the character of Atlantic Richfield, the huge oil company better known as ARCO, was shaped by its longtime CEO, Robert O. Anderson. A product of the Great Books program at the University of Chicago, Anderson made his company a patron of the arts and education. Employees are encouraged to contribute to social betterment projects, and its annual report is titled, "To Make a Difference: Arco and Society." In an industry where most companies are heavily slanted toward the S and T poles, ARCO has a distinct NF cast to its character.[10]

The current leader leaves the last mark, and it may be a very deep one. Jack Welch is doing that at GE and, to a lesser extent, John Sculley has done that at Apple. Although in some organizations, the current leader's mark is definitive, the last mark can prove to be as ephemeral as writing in the sand—and the organization in the end can revert to its earlier character as soon as the leader departs. United Air Lines has done that, after its temporary experiment with diversification and characterological change, when Richard Ferris bundled it together with Hertz and two hotel chains as Allegis, a travel conglomerate.

Another factor in an organization's character is its history. Some companies have long traditions, while others don't. If the company has never had an unprofitable quarter in three decades, or if the company has had to struggle back several times from the edge of bankruptcy, its character may be affected. If a company's scientist wins the Nobel Prize, or if a company is rocked by a defense scandal, these historical occurrences will probably affect its character. Certainly the character of the old Bell System was shaped by its history as a protected monopoly, just as after 1984 the character of each of its regional components was shaped by the historical trauma of its breakup.

Taken together, these factors make it possible for competitors in the same industry to have rather different characters. Take Citibank and Morgan Guarantee Trust, two of America's most celebrated financial institutions. The former is fast-track, risk-taking, exciting. It expanded substantially during the 1980s, issuing millions of credit cards, moving into new regions, developing new services. Citibank is extraverted–sensing–thinking–perceiving, ESTP. Morgan Guarantee Trust, on the other hand, has only three public offices, sticks to its specialized business of providing special services to very large accounts, and emphasizes what it calls *relationship banking*. Morgan is introverted–sensing–feeling–judging, or ISFJ. It's no accident that people considered Citibank a star and Morgan too old-fashioned during the go-go years of the early 1980s—or that in 1991, after the banking system has gone through the ringer, Morgan looks solid and Citibank is in trouble. Once again, we see that there is no good or bad character—just character that fits or fails to fit a particular situation.

Organizational Character and the Organizational Life Cycle

In addition to the factors listed above, there is a characterological overlay that comes from the stage an organization is in relative to its life cycle. Is it an energetic start-up, or is it a middle-aged institution? The same organization will probably change its character in subtle ways over time.[11]

Whatever the founder's personal character, there is often something introverted about the dream out of which a newly born organization grows. It exists inside that founding dreamer, after all. This introverted quality may pervade the new organization for a while, but as the organization develops into a venture, it moves outward into the world. It is looking for customers, clients, investors, collaborators, employees—and it must be at least somewhat extraverted to succeed in finding them.

The early phases of the life cycle are seed times for something larger. Actuality may not be anything very impressive, but there may be great possibility. So there is often an intuitive quality about the organization's youth. Things haven't been worked out in detail—there's only a design, a model, a pattern, or process. The very conduct of the undertaking is likely to have an intuitive quality, with decisions being made on the spur of the moment and with things being run in a seat-of-the-pants fashion.

But if the venture is successful and the organization grows, things get more and more complicated. Ad hoc decisions begin to contradict one another, and catch-as-catch-can practices begin to be inadequate to the situation. Policies are needed, and systems of various sorts become necessary. The founder's desk drawers give way to filing systems, his or her PC is replaced by the corporate data bank, and the old egalitarian spirit begins to disappear as an increasingly complex system of roles and ranks develops. A more detail-oriented style is needed, and the organization's character begins to shift toward the sensing end of the spectrum.

From this point on, the organization's developmental path gets to be harder to predict. For one thing, as it differentiates into diverse departments and product groups, different functional characters will begin to coexist under the same roof. For another thing, there is likely to be a slow oscillation throughout the organization's history between the forces of extraversion and introversion (what the market wants versus who we really are) and between sensing and intuition (what we do or make versus what we *could* do or make).

When you add to these factors the influence of history and a succession of leaders, you see that the organization's character is certainly going to change over the years. And with all the variables at work, you can see that the changes are going to be somewhat unpredictable. No two organizations follow the same path, and any given organization may have a specific character only for a while. The important point is that at any given time, an organization will have a particular character, which will to a large extent shape its destiny. That being so, let us turn now to the question of how to recognize the organization's character.

Chapter Two

Identifying Organizational Character

Organizational Character—the Spirit and the Letter

One of the things that drew me to the idea of organizational character was that it could be readily described, categorized, and identified. While the instrument for identifying organizational character appears at the end of this book, it is more important to understand what lies behind it than to be familiar with the instrument itself. If you understand the spirit that animates the *Organizational Character Index*, you will find yourself doing many organizational character assessments in your head rather than on paper.

Identifying an Organization as Extraverted or Introverted

Remember that extraversion (E) and introversion (I) refer to two types of organizational orientation, two different locations for organizational "reality," and two different sources of organizational energy. Here are some of the ways to determine which type of orientation predominates in a given organization.

- *Extraverted organizations* turn outward when looking for indications as to what direction they should take. Their strategy is usually dictated by their reading of market conditions or what their customers are looking for. Before preparing to launch a new effort, they are likely to arm themselves with surveys and expert analyses.

Introverted organizations, on the other hand, turn inward under these same circumstances. Their strategy tends to be dictated by their own technical capabilities or their leaders' ideas or values. When they prepare to redefine strategy, they are likely to review the organization's recent history and to discuss the options as those present see them.

> *Example:* Both Ford Motor Company and General Motors have recently put much emphasis on cutting costs and improving quality. But introverted General Motors has done it by analyzing its own internal processes and automating them, largely overlooking the lessons to be learned in its joint venture with Toyota. The more extraverted Ford has spent much time studying how its Japanese partner, Mazda, has cut costs and improved quality.

In recent years, in fact, the quality improvement movement has swung from the introverted to the extraverted end of the spectrum. "Quality has moved from a set of numbers on a chart to what feels right to the customer," according to Vanderbilt University's operations management specialist, Joseph Blackburn.[1]

- *Extraverted organizations* can act quickly, sometimes even before they have taken the time to fully understand what they are up against. They can be impatient with efforts to get more information or to improve the way it is interpreted. Rather than exploring their options privately and then committing to one course of action, extraverted organizations often experiment with several lines of action and then let the results decide the question.

Introverted organizations, on the contrary, usually try to avoid sudden actions—though they may be forced into them by events. Their preference is to take in and interpret information carefully and to explore their options in detail before any action is taken. Sometimes this drive to understand-before-you-act can slip over into understand-instead-of-act.

> *Example:* Research-based start-up companies may carry the introverted tendencies of the laboratory over into the marketplace and spend so long experimenting with and refining their product that they get bypassed by larger, more extraverted companies that are willing to try out a product even though there are dozens of fascinating unanswered questions about it.

- *Extraverted organizations* often have *porous* or accessible boundaries to their decision-making structure. Things may be kept private for reasons of competitive advantage or legality, but if one wanted to watch decisions take shape, one could probably figure out how to do it. The possibility of influencing the outcome varies with position and power, of course, but in extraverted organizations influence is fairly widespread. There are likely to be periodic updates as the discussions continue, and possible outcomes may even be circulated for reaction. Collaboration is often attempted and consensus frequently sought before decisions are reached.

Introverted organizations, on the other hand, make decisions behind closed doors—not just of necessity, but by preference. It is often hard to know how decisions are made or how one might have input into those decisions. Collaborative decision making is seldom attempted, and consensus is seldom sought—although there may be attempts to build a consensus after the decision has been reached. While the deciding process is going on, little is said. Then, one day, a decision is announced. Some introverted organizations acknowledge these matters humorously: At M&M Mars, a notoriously secretive company, headquarters is jokingly referred to as "The Kremlin."

> *Example:* Most introverted companies symbolize and reinforce this aspect of their character with separate executive offices. Compare Honda Motors' extraverted approach, as described by Richard Pascale in his recent study, *Managing On The Edge* (1990):
>
>> [The company's founder] made sure that there were always fewer desks and offices available than executives. As a result, desks had to be shared. With no office or desk to call one's own, top executives were forced to be out and about. They became, in effect, itinerant facilitators, problem solvers, and on-the-scene decision makers. To this day, the top forty directors and managing directors of Honda are housed in a single open area with only six individual desks and five large circular conference tables.

• *Extraverted organizations* depend heavily on conversations and meetings. Oral communication is the norm, even for complex or important decisions. Written communications are considered unnecessary and tend to be mistrusted because you never know how they'll be taken and because they're perceived to cast ideas in concrete. The pace of words at an extraverted organization's meetings is faster than at an introverted organization's, and God forbid there should be silences!

Introverted organizations usually rely heavily on written communications, even between people who often see one another face-to-face. Written communications permit more precision and give everyone time to think things over before a reply is made or an action taken. Meetings are sometimes undervalued because it's hard for people to know what to think when others are there, talking and interrupting. The meetings of introverted organizations may be cryptic, full of pregnant silences, and hard to follow unless one is in the know.[2]

Example: The small, extraverted start-up company is probably
going to depend heavily on oral communication and spontaneous
meetings to get its business done—even in communicating with
bigger, introverted organizations, where it is the norm to put everything into writing. The fact of that difference will convince the
extraverted company that the introverted one is "bureaucratic." But
the same extraverted start-up will need to become more introverted
(and to put more in writing) as it grows. That necessity will be
interpreted by old-timers as a "loss of character" and as unfortunate
and (mistakenly) even unnecessary.

• *Extraverted organizations*, even when they are large, encourage collaboration between areas. Since turf-building is a general human weakness,
they have turf problems. But their expectation is that people should be
willing to let others see what they are doing and to take suggestions about
how to do it better. Collaborative projects are fairly common in these
organizations, and project teams are a natural way to solve a new problem
or launch a new effort.

Introverted organizations, unless they are pretty small, tend to be
somewhat compartmentalized. There is a belief that people are most
productive if they can be given tasks and then left alone to do them without
much interruption. This makes collaboration feel a little contrived, but it
also leads to the development of excellent specialized functions—highly
professional accounting or design, for example. This gain is partly offset by
the idea that such tasks should belong to the doers, leading to the development
of various fiefdoms. Something done in one of these turf areas is expected
to be finished and then shown or passed on to people in other areas. You
don't touch other peoples' projects until they invite you to.

Example: Ford's interdisciplinary team that designed the Taurus in
record time, like those at IBM that designed the PC (and, more
recently, the laptop) show an extraverted style; different functions
work together to build their perspectives into the output. These
companies had traditionally relied on an introverted strategy, which
involved designing a car or a computer with no concern for its
manufacturability or marketability, then "throwing it over the wall" to
manufacturing, who grumbled that the design would never work, and
then handing off the product to salespeople who had to figure out
how to sell it to people who might have wanted something else.

• *Extraverted organizations*, during difficult times, will often bring in
outsiders to provide new ideas or to help them evaluate or deal with whatever mess they are in. They are more likely than introverted organizations
to seek input from the people out in the field (i.e., those closest to the external

world) when things take a turn for the worse. They try their own ideas out on focus groups of their customers. Organizational celebrations are likely to involve outsiders, both from other organizations and from the community. Their definition of the organizational "family" is a very inclusive one.

Introverted organizations, on the other hand, circle the wagons whenever there is trouble. When they need to find new ideas, they look first to their own experts; when ideas do come from outside, they have to win approval at lengthy internal discussions.[3] (NIH, or Not Invented Here, is an introverted disease.) When they want to celebrate, they do it within the *immediate* family. When they want to renew themselves, they take the corporate executives off on a retreat and resist the idea that they need an outsider to help them facilitate it.

> *Example:* Compare Detroit's traditional (though currently changing) introverted automotive design process with that at extraverted Honda, where all designers spend a full quarter of their time attending dealer meetings and automotive conventions so that they can see first hand what the public is looking for.

Below is a summary of the characteristics of extraverted versus introverted organizations. On the basis of these descriptions, would you say that your organization was extraverted (E) or introverted (I)?

Extraverted Organizations	*Introverted Organizations*
Have open boundaries	Have closed boundaries
Allow access to decision making	Prevent access to decision making
Collaborate on decisions	Reach consensus after a decision is made
Act quickly	Respond only after study
Experiment with several possible lines of action	Explore options in detail, then try one line of action
Trust oral communication	Trust written communication
Encourage interdepartmental cooperation	Experience interdepartmental mistrust
Turn outside for guidance	Insist guidance must come from within
Seek assistance when in trouble	Circle the wagons when in trouble
Invite outsiders to celebrations	Keep celebrations "in the family"
Have as a motto, "The answer is out there—we just have to find it"	Have as a motto, "The answer's within—we just have to figure it out"

Identifying an Organization as Sensing or Intuitive

Remember that sensing (S) and intuition (N) refer to two different styles of perception, two different ways of paying attention to the world and taking in information. Here are some ways to determine which basic style of perception predominates in a given organization.

• *Sensing organizations* are focused on the actualities of the situations encountered in their business. In production, they are good with specifics and particulars. The great German architect, Mies van der Rohe, seemed to be speaking for such organizations when he said, "God is in the details." In their internal affairs, they can maintain order within large bodies of data. Their filing systems and data banks are highly organized. Their common operations are covered by standard procedures, whether they involve maintenance, accounting, security, shipping, or MIS. They sometimes achieve this order, however, at the expense of a clear sense of where things are going.

Intuitive organizations are looser. They look at situations and see the big picture rather than the details, and as a result, the details sometimes get lost. But they are more likely to see what is under the surface, what is about to happen or what could be done. They tend to be oriented toward possibilities and to regard actualities as little more than the way things happen to be now. Intuitive organizations can often be found working on a whole new way to do something or to capitalize on an emerging situation. They are fascinated with developments and relatively bored with day-to-day routine.

> *Example:* Apple Computer has grown incredibly fast by responding to its own intuitive visions of what people need. Its CEO, John Sculley, has said, "The best way to be ready for the future is to invent it." (He has also admitted that when he got to Apple, he found that people often didn't bother to answer or return phone calls.) A sensing powerhouse like Procter & Gamble, on the other hand, is famous for conducting exhaustive statistical market surveys before launching any new product—and you can bet that it has a never-fail phone-answering system.

• *Sensing organizations* have their own characteristic way of planning and implementing change. They do it incrementally: With their respect for the actual and the situational, they see change as improvement of what already exists. They may be innovative, but the innovation tends to be in the details rather than in the overall design. At one end of the spectrum, sensing organizations may tinker with things; at the other end, they may have continuous improvement programs. In either case, they believe in taking things a step at a time.

Intuitive organizations, on the other hand, are likely to innovate more holistically. They tend to view change transformationally rather than incrementally and so are more receptive to from-the-ground-up changes than sensing organizations are. They like to begin with the *paradigm*, or the basic reality behind a situation, and to focus on changing how people think, not just how they act. Intuitive organizations are often attracted to radically new technologies or ideologies, showing an interest in trends and megatrends and to be energized by attuning themselves to the future. Sensing organizations are energized by the present—which they call reality. They are likely to regard intuitive organizations as too idealistic or impractical, while intuitive organizations regard sensing ones as overcautious or stuck-in-the-mud.

> *Example:* At most companies, the research and development department is intuitive, while manufacturing is sensing. Planning is intuitive, and administration is sensing. The organizational development group is intuitive, and the personnel department, to whom they sometimes report, is likely to be sensing. No wonder these different groups carry on such a tug-of-war with one another.

• *Sensing organizations*, when preparing for change, create their picture of the future based on past experience and on projections extrapolated from recent and present data. With their faith in cause-and-effect relationships, sensing organizations tend to view these projections as reliable and solid. Such projections are turned into targets or objectives that are often quantified, after which the organization makes a plan for getting there. Until there is a plan, the sensing organization feels that nothing has been decided. Once there is a plan, however, "everything is set." The pitfall of planning for the sensing organization is that the wonderfully designed plan may be nothing more than a path to yesterday. For the data that is so dear to sensing organizations often proves to be an unreliable guide to tomorrow, and those sensible extrapolations of current trends are more and more often turning out to be mirages that disappear as one approaches.

Intuitive organizations, on the other hand, are not so often surprised by sharp discontinuities between today and tomorrow. (They don't necessarily *like* such breaks, since tomorrow may look pretty dark. But they believe that change naturally comes in big jumps.) They are much likelier to use their imagination in constructing the future and to regard it as theirs to create. Intuitive organizations are attracted to the idea of visioning and are as energized by visions-of-the-future as sensing organizations are by a solid grasp of the facts of the present and experience from the past. Intuitive organizations are likely to view the sensing tendency to be unimpressed with visioning as a sign of unimaginativeness or conservatism.

> *Example:* While attempting to become different, AT&T has tried to change its service by improving basic services that already exist; MCI, on the other hand, has sought to improve its position by transforming the whole technology of long-distance service. Sensing organizations say, "If it ain't broke, don't fix it." Intuitive organizations say, "If you see a better way to do it, go for it."

• *Sensing organizations* try to break down large changes into little steps and prefer to break complex situations into their component parts. In each case, the organization feels more at home with the particulars than with unique wholes.

Intuitive organizations, on the other hand, gravitate toward wholes and consider a focus on particulars as oversimplification. In complex situations, therefore, the two kinds of organizations take different paths: The sensing organization seeks to simplify things by reducing them to their component elements; the intuitive organization seeks to grasp them whole and work with them that way.

> *Example:* McDonald's has made a fetish out of reducing the production of hamburgers to a step-by-step science, while Domino's Pizza has been a much more hit-or-miss company based on a single, inventive idea: People will pay to get fast delivery of home-delivered food.

• *Sensing organizations* trust experience. The tried-and-true appeals to them, whether unconsciously followed as a technical solution or con-sciously embraced as a tradition. Status and power in such organizations usually go to people with experience in the organization, or at least in the business or industry that the organization is affiliated with. Skill and competence are defined in terms of experience, and there is a tendency to organize roles and structures as bodies of similarly experienced people. That means that functional groupings—all the engineers together in the engineering department, all the marketers together in the marketing de-partment—are the preferred form of organization.

Intuitive organizations, on the other hand, view experience as a double-edged sword because of their vision of a future different from the past.

Experience is seen as useful because skills are useful, but it is also mistrusted as a justification for not doing things differently. Because of its tendency to deal with situations as unique wholes, an intuitive organization will often establish interfunctional groupings to get a particular task done. These groups may be ad hoc project teams or semipermanent strategic business units. And within such groupings, power and status do not necessarily go to the most experienced people but rather to the most brilliant people, the best leaders, or the most highly motivated people.

> *Example:* The regional phone companies, the so-called Baby Bells,
> have all been struggling to abandon the hierarchical, by the book,
> sensing approach that characterized the old Bell system and to
> develop the lighter footed, more future-oriented intuitive spirit
> of innovation.

• *Sensing organizations*, for all the reasons already described, put a lot of faith in policies, regulations, and standard operating procedures. New hires are socialized into the organization by learning "how we do things here," and doing things the right way means doing them the approved way.

Intuitive organizations may also have policies, but they are likelier to be tied to the vision and to the belief system of the organization rather than to its past and its time-tested practices. New hires are socialized by learning "what we believe," and doing things the right way means doing them in the right spirit.

> *Example:* When René McPherson took over as the new CEO at Dana
> Corporation, he inherited a company so sensing that it was choking
> on its own countless regulations. Seeking to develop a more intuitive
> character, he assembled the corporation's top officials and described
> to them the changes he was going to make in operating procedures
> and policies. On the table next to him was a stack of company policy
> manuals two feet high. At the dramatic height of his address, he
> turned, and with a swing of his arm, knocked them all to the floor. He
> held up a single sheet of paper on which were written his principles.
> He explained that people could understand these principles and make
> their decisions based upon them. As the years passed, Dana became
> more and more intuitive—something of an anomaly in the auto parts
> business—and very successful.

Below is a summary of the characteristics of sensing versus intuitive organizations. On the basis of these descriptions, would you say that your organization was sensing (S) or intuitive (N)?

Sensing Organizations	Intuitive Organizations
Are at their best with detail	Are at their best with the big picture
Can handle masses of data	Can spot emerging trends
Prefer solid routines	Are a little careless about routines
Prefer incremental change	Prefer transformational change
Make improvements	Change "paradigms"
See intuitive organizations as lost in the clouds	See sensing organizations as stuck in the mud
See the future as an extension of the present	Believe the future can be created
Emphasize targets and plans	Emphasize purposes and vision
Trust experience and authority	Trust insight and creativity
Tend to organize functionally	Often use cross-functional teams
Have as a motto, "Change the structure"	Have as a motto, "Change the belief systems"

Identifying an Organization as Thinking or Feeling

Remember that thinking (T) and feeling (F) refer to different ways that organizations make decisions—two different ways of judging situations and processing information.[4] Here are some of the ways to determine which style predominates in a given organization.

• *Thinking organizations* attack problems with an arsenal of principles. Whether business principles, professional principles, scientific principles, or moral principles, they are applied more or less impartially and logically. Special circumstances are not given very much weight, because it is the categorical identity of something and not its peculiarities that count.

Feeling organizations, on the other hand, are not driven by impersonal principles but rather by values that have a strong personal component. At the heart of decisions and actions is more likely to be what-we-care-about than what-is-logical. Policies and plans in the feeling organization have more of a focus on the people who have to carry them out, while in the thinking organization they will be justified by the outcome, regardless of the human implications.

Example: The employee assistance and employee relations groups are feeling-oriented and often find themselves at odds with the personnel departments to which they often report and with which they have to work. Personnel tends to be a policy-driven record-keeping (thinking) organization.

• *Thinking organizations* are most at home in dealing with the nonhuman aspects of situations, often acting as though the human dimension to an issue simply was not there. This tendency is sometimes justified by the fact that many thinking organizations are concerned with products or services in which the human element is a minimal component. But that justification is only partly valid, since it is human employees who make the product or deliver the service. And the customers, no matter how technical their needs, are human beings. When they must deal directly with human issues, thinking organizations often fall back on principles like fairness, honesty, loyalty, and responsibility.

Feeling organizations, on the other hand, emphasize the human element in its rawer form and view such principles as pale substitutes for a real sense of people and their individual needs. The internal management style of the feeling organization is not necessarily "nicer" than the thinking organization's—fairness and loyalty are, after all, "nice" ideas. The feeling style simply deals with people as people and with their different needs, value systems, personality traits, and dreams.

> *Example:* Hewlett-Packard and Pitney Bowes are two companies considered to be well managed and good places to work. Hewlett-Packard is a thinking company that has been shaped by its original business: test and measurement equipment. Policies are sensible and people are treated in a logical way, but a cool impersonality pervades the company. At Pitney Bowes the business isn't so different, but the character is more dominated by feeling. Effective employee relations are the key, and the company holds annual "jobholders meetings," comparable to a stockholders meeting, where employees engage in face-to-face debate with the company's leadership. There is also a Council of Personnel Relations to deal with ongoing employee issues.

• *Thinking organizations* distrust "merely personal" issues and consequently lack effective ways to integrate them into the organization's affairs. (For that reason, they may very well operate powerfully in an unconscious way under the surface of situations, while everyone denies that they should or are influencing anything.) The thinking organization attempts to generalize everything and to resist individual answers. It also resists getting personal in discussing issues or studying problems.

Feeling organizations do not necessarily get into personal issues in the sense of invading privacy, but they take it for granted that good solutions to problems must take personal considerations into account. *Good* in this

sense means *good for the people involved* as well as good in its strategic outcome. For this reason, discussions and analyses are likely to get into
personal areas. Since feeling in this sense does not mean *emotion*, the feeling
organization is not necessarily a place where there are tears and yelling.[5]
Feeling simply means that considerations of the heart are taken at least as
seriously as those of the head.

> *Example:* Delta Airlines has long been famous for its warm service
> and good employee relations; even in this day of high turnover, it
> has many long-term employees who like its family atmosphere.
> TWA and Continental, on the other hand, have impersonal operating
> styles that have been sharpened by recent histories of management-
> employee antagonism. [6]

• *Thinking organizations* may be easygoing or harsh, but in either
case they are likely to have a *critical* climate. That is, since such organizations
see things in terms of ideas and principles, they treat every situation as one
that should be looked at critically. Designs are well done or poorly done.
Plans are clearly articulated or not. Management techniques are successful or unsuccessful—quality, customer service, leadership, or communication—everything is viewed as though it were a part of a machine that
either does its job or doesn't. In its more benign form, this leads to
painstaking evaluation; in its more extreme form, it leads to condescending
lectures, harsh appraisals, and nasty, even violent, attacks on projects and
people.

Feeling organizations tend to be more supportive and less critical. That
is not to say that angry words don't pass between people at such organizations. It is just that such words don't represent the dominant idea about
how people work best. Feeling organizations attempt to get the best out of
people individually and to work harmoniously together collectively.
Thinking organizations try to get people to do the right or intelligent things
individually and to work efficiently together collectively. In thinking
organizations, people are supposed to accept criticism, no matter how
painful it is because that is how people improve. In feeling organizations,
people are supposed to accept criticism because it is how people talk when
they are frustrated or upset. But that state is supposed to pass, and then
everyone is supposed to work together to make things turn out well. An
implicit goal of the feeling organization is harmony, while the thinking
organization implicitly aims at efficiency.

> *Example:* The thinking–feeling difference often stands in the way
> of an organizational development department's effectiveness in a
> manufacturing or financial company. The OD mission, involving as it

does human issues, is feeling in nature. It often emphasizes values and the clarification of those values as a starting place for organizational changes. The business of manufacture or finance is thinking. Values are seldom the starting points for action. Problems are. Changes are meant to solve problems, and "values" are likely to strike the thinking organization as beside the point. The misunderstandings that can develop between these two divergent points of view are huge, and it is usually the OD department that loses. In fact, it is often the feeling-based group that loses out in a head-to-head with a thinking-based group, because thinking sounds so much more logical and sensible that it's hard for the feeling group to justify itself in terms that the thinking-based group can accept.

A summary of the characteristics of thinking versus intuitive organizations is shown below. On the basis of these descriptions, would you say that your organization was thinking (T) or feeling (F)?

Thinking Organizations	*Feeling Organizations*
Make decisions based on principles	Make decisions based on values
Think in terms of rules and exceptions	Think in terms of particular human situations
Value what-is-logical	Value what-we-care-about
Emphasize the objective	Emphasize the people
Believe criticism leads to efficiency	Believe support leads to effectiveness
Encourage employees to live up to expectations	Encourage employees to do their best
Are a social machine	Are a social community
Have as a motto, "Do the right (or intelligent) thing"	Have as a motto, "Work well together"

Identifying an Organization as Judging or Perceiving

Remember that judging (J) and perceiving (P) refer to two different emphases that organizations demonstrate in dealing with the world. Judging organizations tend to use thinking or feeling, which are the judging functions, to deal with their outer world, while perceiving organizations use sensing or intuition, the so-called perceiving functions, in dealing with their outer world. Here are some of the ways to determine which style predominates in a given organization.

• *Judging organizations* prefer to reach firm decisions, and their management system is likely to be oriented toward decision making. If the judging is of the *thinking* variety, the decisions are reached by using the principles of the head, while in *feeling* organizations, the values of the heart are more important. In either case, things move toward a decision as water flows toward the sea. If decisions become impossible because of conflict or ambiguity, everyone is uncomfortable.

Perceiving organizations, on the other hand, do not value decisions so highly. They may even be avoided if people feel it limits discussion or precludes further input; people often become uncomfortable if they feel someone is pushing them for a decision. Perceiving organizations act as though they were in a constant state of fact finding and climate assessment.

> *Example:* Part of the perennial conflict between the line functions and the support staff in big organizations is that the former have a strong judging orientation, while the latter are often perceiving. The support organizations tend to have more reflective missions and emphasize situational complexity, while those of the operating groups emphasize action and would happily settle for a quick-and-dirty solution to the organization's problems.

• *Judging organizations* sometimes run into trouble because they have made a decision prematurely and on the basis of too little evidence. Intelligence-gathering activities tend to be weak or perfunctory, and preconceptions too often pass for information. Judging organizations need to push themselves to stay open to the world, to challenge their assumptions by studying organizations that are very different, and to count to ten before they act.

Perceiving organizations, on the contrary, usually run into trouble because they have unduly delayed or completely avoided a decision that should have been made. They often lack the structures and functional roles that make decision making easier. They sometimes use their egalitarian values and their preference for consensus building as excuses for not forcing themselves to fish or cut bait. They need to question those excuses and face the price they pay for their free-wheeling openness to "a little more testing of the waters" and "just a little more discussion."

> *Example:* Research groups tend to have a perceiving character, and manufacturing groups are almost always judging. The latter are likely to grow impatient with the way that the former keeps modifying the

design, even after it has been delivered for actual manufacture. More generally, staff groups are often more perceiving than line groups, since their function is to generate and interpret data—and since there is always new data being discovered. The line group will want an answer ("Just tell us yes or no, for heaven's sake!") and will talk about how impractical the staff group is—"This is the real world, you know, not some ivory tower!" The staff group, on the other hand, is likely to feel that the line operation cares more for answers than whether they are right. The conflict exists throughout the organizational world.

• *Judging organizations* prefer to define things as clearly as possible— standards and procedures on the thinking side, and expectations and concerns on the feeling side. Both types of judging organizations share the belief that by spelling things out, they remove most sources of misunderstanding and reasons for poor performance.

Perceiving organizations, on the other hand, believe that such specificity cuts off creativity and limits freedom. On the intuitive end of the perceiving spectrum, defining everything very carefully is avoided for fear of foreclosing possibilities and hampering the power of the vision. On the sensing end of the spectrum, such definition is felt to get in the way of the instinctive skill that the experienced person brings to a task. The latter group fears that the definers will "talk us to death," while the former group fears that the definers will "kill our spirit."

> *Example:* As noted earlier, Citibank and Morgan Guarantee Trust are worlds apart characterologically. This is nowhere truer than on the *judging–perceiving* scale. Morgan Guarantee Trust Company is famous for its deliberate and conservative approach to banking. Citicorp, on the other hand, is equally famous for its free-wheeling, keep-all-the-possibilities-open approach to the same business. The former exudes the air of establishment formality, while one of its executives said of the latter:
>
> > This place is organized chaos. We start a lot of things and only ten to twenty percent of them survive.... A lot of other companies with a more rigorous management style wouldn't allow that. But around here, we build things and blow them up, then start again.[7]

• *Judging organizations* often have a moralistic streak about them, for their decision-making and closure-seeking style naturally divides things into yes and no, good and bad, wise and foolish, go and no-go. Having made the decision, they have a tendency to want to impose it on others. Having decided to head north, they find themselves bumping into everyone who is heading south. And it is a short step from deciding what "our" way will be to talking about the "right" way to do things.

Perceiving organizations stay more undefined and loose and are therefore less likely to view others moralistically—except, of course, in their belief that judging organizations are uptight and no fun.[8] But in their very "unjudging" quality, perceiving organizations can find themselves adrift. In spite of their bias toward fluidity, they may need to find some firm ground and take a stand on it.

> *Example:* ROLM Corporation, one of the leaders in the field of telephone exchange equipment, was famous for its easygoing perceiving openness and lack of formal standards. It was an early proponent of flextime. One of its official principles was to avoid bureaucracy, and it was famous for its Friday afternoon beer busts. Then in the mideighties, it was bought by a decidedly judging company, IBM. IBM has formal policies—and not so many years earlier, an official dress code of dark tie and white shirt. Not too surprisingly, the acquisition has been a painful one for people on both sides.

Below is presented a summary of the characteristics of judging versus perceiving organizations. On the basis of these descriptions, would you say that your organization was judging (J) or perceiving (P)?

Judging Organizations	*Perceiving Organizations*
Drive toward decisions	Keep options open and seek more information
May be weak in information gathering	May be weak in decision making
Set clear, specific standards	Set general standards
Define lots of things in detail	Leave many things vague and undefined
Are often moralistic	Are loose and fairly tolerant
Have as a motto, "Fish or cut bait"	Have as a motto, "Don't miss an opportunity"

The Character of Your Organization

As you have read through these descriptions, you have been asked to reflect on the character of some organization that you know well. Before going further, sum up what you have discovered. What are the four letters you chose as the best descriptors of your organization? Was it E or I, S or N, T or F, J or P? Render the answer as a four-letter typological code.

Your organization is

Turn to Chapter 3 now to read the description of this character type.

Chapter Three

The Sixteen Types of Organizational Character

The sixteen different types of organizational character are described in this chapter. Find the one that corresponds to the four letters that you believe best characterize your organization.[1] Remember that the character of your particular department or division may be different from that of the organization and that the smaller unit is also more likely to have a distinctive and readily identifiable character than is a very large one.

The ESTJ Organization

Extraverted—focuses outward, responds to external stimuli
Sensing—concerns itself with actualities, attends to details
Thinking—depends on impersonal procedures and principles
Judging—likes things spelled out and definite, seeks closure

Whatever its size—and ESTJ organizations can sometimes grow very big— this kind of organization has an administrative or an operational flavor to it. It runs its show and does it well. It has rules. There are clear responsibilities and definite procedures, and they are consistent and logical. Details are attended to. The bottom line is what counts, and there is a distrust of the abstract, the soft, or the unquantifiable. Time is money. There is a no-nonsense quality to the organization that is reassuring—but also limiting.

That same characteristic suggests that whatever dissenting voices there may be are at best quibblers and at worst troublemakers. So ESTJ organizations do not get the benefit of alternative points of view very often.

The ESTJ organization tends to be hierarchical. Status counts for a lot, and turf is important. Credentials are taken seriously, and the standards of the organization are likely to be both firm and orthodox. Standard operating procedures are used to hold variance to a minimum. There is an acceptable way to do everything, and that way is generally thought to be fairly obvious. Kooks and weirdos might do it some very different way, "but here at Techtocorp, we think that it is just common sense to...." Compliance with regulations is insured by supervision or inspection, and everything possible is standardized.

With its logical procedures, the ESTJ organization coordinates different efforts well. It sticks to schedules. It works out its plans carefully and doesn't spin off wild, risky ventures. Perceptions are tested before they are acted on—unless they fit with the collective wisdom and then they may be followed unthinkingly. The "right" kind of people feel they belong here and that their efforts will be rewarded.

The ESTJ organization is solid, but the flip side is its rigidity. It is not very responsive to individual differences and may be impatient with prima donnas and superstars who are likely to be happier elsewhere. (Sad to say, even some very mild individualists find themselves called prima donnas.) In sending such folks packing or not hiring them in the first place, the organization loses out on a good deal of creativity.

Whatever its size, the ESTJ organization acts like an institution that has been there for a while and means to stay. It is most at home in an environment that is not changing too fast, for it doesn't like to make fast turns or sudden reversals. It may have trouble spotting trends quickly, though it can get everyone focused on the trend when it finally does. It isn't likely to be very good at developing radically innovative new products or services, though it delivers whatever it does do efficiently and on time.

Denial can be a problem with this kind of organization—denial that anything has really changed, then denial that the time-tested ways are inadequate. When denial breaks down, people become disoriented. This smoothly run organization can turn into chaos almost overnight.

The people who fit best in the ESTJ organization like things to be predictable. They are realistic people who aren't easily swept away by hunches or sudden insights. They mistrust feelings and often pass off a concern or an issue as "merely personal." They like interactions within the organization to be a little formal, and they have a soft spot for traditions. Deferring to superiors is not uncomfortable for them, and with the passing years, they grow into the tried and true workers who can be counted on to know the best way to deal with practical difficulties.

ESTJ organizations have a tendency to preserve and protect things—to insure that things will happen as promised. That is their manner, but it can also be their business—that is, such organizations are often found in fields where the task is to establish something and then keep it there.

Any organization may go through a sort of ESTJ phase when it is coming out of a change or riding the calm waters between changes, for the ESTJ way is one of consolidating, system building, implementing, producing, anchoring, stabilizing, and regulating. As means to ends, these are essential qualities. Many other kinds of organizations fail because they lack them. But as ends in themselves, these qualities can spell trouble if the environment is changing quickly and constantly.

It is difficult to change the ESTJ organization, partly because any habit is hard to break and ESTJ's thrive on habit, but also because the ESTJ organization takes its own collective wisdom so seriously. Innovative ideas usually come from individuals or small teams, and ESTJ organizations are likely to distrust individualism and little "maverick" groups. Furthermore, ESTJ organizations are highly prescriptive and full of expectations: People should do their duty, subordinate their personal needs to the general good, and act the right way. People who don't do that are mistrusted—hence, the them versus us mentality. The result is that the ESTJ organization is a hard nut to crack.

Many of the big manufacturing companies are ESTJ companies. So are the manufacturing or operations sectors in many large companies. IBM, as it has grown less introverted in recent years, is one. So are some of the regional phone companies, which have also learned that they have to pay attention to their markets. It's a similar story with Kodak. In fact, many of the giant corporations used to be ISTJ, but then the new competition appeared, and everyone is hustling to become more extraverted.

The ESFJ Organization

Extraverted—focuses outward, responds to external stimuli
Sensing—concerns itself with actualities, attends to details
Feeling—reaches conclusions on the basis of values and beliefs
Judging—likes things spelled out and definite, seeks closure

The ESFJ organization is outward-looking and self-confident. Often found in trade or some field that requires the marketing of a service, it is an organization that listens well to the people in its external environment. As long as the data falls within a range of expected response, the ESFJ organization will catch it and act upon it. If the data is unexpected or unique, however, the organization may fail to see its significance. So the shadow side that an ESFJ organization shows is a tendency to turn its back on the client sending signals that are too unconventional.

The same two-sidedness exists within the ESFJ organization. Even if it is large, there can be a family aspect to the organization. Company events can be warm and enjoyable. It takes good care of its loyal people. But it expects loyalty and defines it in a fairly circumscribed way. Someone who falls outside what may be a fairly narrow range of defined loyalty may be sent packing. The same fate may occur to people whose ideas or standards or appearance is strange or substandard. Consensus is important to the ESFJ organization, and it reaps the benefits of being able to generate it. But if it fails, it can have trouble.

The world in which an ESFJ organization exists is one that is often seen as being threatened by deterioration or dissipation. The organization is, by character, vigilant to guard against loss—its own, or that of its clients. It is trustee-minded, solid, and dependable. Economic responsibility is a very important value, and ownership is taken very seriously. The organization saves things: data, records, materials. It passes on traditions well.

ESFJ organizations are good at routine operations, and they usually perform at a high standard. They mistrust the abstract and the overly complex. Wherever things can be somewhat standardized, wherever commitment and hard work will produce results, wherever a sincere desire to serve its clients well is enough, the ESFJ organization will shine. It meets deadlines. Its standard operating procedures insure reliable output. Its solid hierarchy guarantees responsible oversight of what is done. Impatient with too much processing, it can be counted on to reach a decision. It has a clear agenda.

But, again, all this has a reverse side. The solidity can also be slow moving and the standardized procedures can be rigid when the organization is confronted with a novel situation. Simple reliability is not enough when the problem is too complex. The hierarchy can turn into turf-guarders when a new configuration is called for. And the traditional knowledge, so effective in dealing with routine matters, proves inadequate when confronted with new demands from either without or within.

The ESFJ organization is likely to be a pleasant one to work in. People are friendly, and there is a sense of belonging. Role descriptions will generally be clear, although there may be a ring of responsibilities around the edge of the role that exceed what many employees can accomplish. There are likely to be gratifying rituals to mark occasions and anniversaries in the collective (and individual) life cycle. Those who have worked there for a while are ready to coach those who haven't, and a prospective mentor is not too far away.

But the organization is not very flexible or ready to take risks. Leadership prefers to adapt what exists rather than create something new and prefers to modify things step by step rather than start over again from scratch. Initiative may be praised, but it is the initiative of the implementer who will just "get out there and do it" rather than the initiative of the creator who wants to do it in a new way. In short, the ESFJ organization is most comfortable in times of relative stability when needs are well defined and the competition does not change very quickly.

Organizations with an ESFJ character include Hallmark Cards, with its tradition of family ownership, and Procter & Gamble, with its heritage of consumer products. So are customer services groups within many companies.

The ENTJ Organization

Extraverted—focuses outward, responds to external stimuli
Intuitive—concerns itself with possibilities, attends to the big picture
Thinking—depends on impersonal procedures and principles
Judging—likes things spelled out and definite, seeks closure

This type of organization takes command of situations and acts decisively. This is both its strength and its weakness. It sets a strategy based on an intuitive grasp of the situation, then goes after its objectives single-mindedly. Willpower rather than sensitivity drives its efforts.

The other side of this strength is an unawareness of the subtler aspects of situations. This can make the ENTJ organization miss subtle clues to difficulties, and it can make it careless about the human side of what it is trying to do. It is particularly impatient with wasted or ill-conceived actions. The ENTJ organization can thus be a little like a battleship: powerful, but tending to overkill.

The heart of this type of organization is its strategy. The ENTJ organization evolves policies that are subordinated to that strategy, expecting people to fit into those policies and to understand their importance. It may not think to *explain* that importance very clearly or often, however.

It is future- and opportunity-oriented in its outlook and goes about its business in an objective way that often sweeps personal issues under the rug. This style is both a strength and a weakness. At its best, the organization is straightforward and unequivocal; at its worst, it is prescriptive and dogmatic, making people fit into a pattern that it has set without their input. The organization can grow very large without losing its focus, and people who fit the organization's design can get a great sense of purpose from participating in it.

This type of organization is often better with strategy—*grand* strategy, sometimes—than it is with tactics or how the strategy is going to be implemented. There is always a model of reality behind the plan of such an organization, and the model often explains how things work. Hence, the organization is often skilled at functional analysis—though not necessarily so good at sequential analysis.

For both its employees and its customers, the ENTJ organization has a tendency to approach situations from what might be called an *engineering* point of view: thinking impersonally of the factors and forces at work, looking for mechanistic solutions, and weighing variables carefully. Needless to say, this approach works best when people are not the problem. This is ironic, because the leaders of the ENTJ organization may themselves be very individualistic and may endorse self-development vociferously, but it is usually their own self-development that they really believe in.

Because the ENTJ organization is likely to be rather simplistic in its notion of people (at least of people who operate from feeling rather than thinking), it is best with situations where a cool, clear, fresh look is needed and with situations that require functional analysis. The ENTJ organization is likely to see such problems everywhere, and once a problem is identified, the machinery starts—even if sometimes the customer tries to say that that isn't the problem.

ENTJ organizations are proactive and decisive, which makes them effective in change situations where clear action is necessary and delay would be damaging. They are good at seeing the issue quickly and turning their vision into action. They can turn chaos into order, although this need to bring order to disorderly situations may be a little overwhelming. Nothing stands in the way of their efforts. They are quite willing to bowl over sacred cows, break taboos, and take a dim view of anything "illogical." Because of those tendencies, they are sometimes insensitive in their communications.

Internally, they often take people for granted—or take for granted that people see why they must do what they are told. Appreciation may be forgotten and efforts unacknowledged. People are supposed to get the *idea* behind the plan, and that is supposed to be enough. If one makes a mistake more than once, the organization will be displeased. There is a tendency to view things as obvious and to dismiss discussion as small talk and a waste of time.

People are expected to be able to engage in fairly heavy verbal give-and-take. Criticism is always considered constructive, and people who are hurt by such criticism don't tend to last very long. Arguments, which to these organizations are merely discussions, can get rough at times, but they are just part of the way decisions are made and differences worked out.

ENTJ organizations plan change well, although they occasionally get caught up in the planning process and carry it on too long. They are not as responsive to subtle cues as they may need to be and are intolerant of confusing or ambiguous signals. Because they hate inefficiency or imprecision, projects that go through a clumsy growth phase may not fare too well with them. They particularly want to be in charge of their destiny, and whenever that control is threatened, the ENTJ organization will be very troubled.

Pepsico might be such a company, with its religion of beating Coke and its use of "The Pepsi challenge" advertising. So, too, might American Airlines, which is pursuing a grand strategy of expansion in an environment where many competitors are vanishing.

The ENFJ Organization

Extraverted—focuses outward, responds to external stimuli
Intuitive—concerns itself with possibilities, attends to the big picture
Feeling—reaches conclusions on the basis of values and beliefs
Judging—likes things spelled out and definite, seeks closure

This type of organization is dynamic and has a positive, energetic style. It handles change better than many other types of organizations, emphasizing the envisioned goal and making sure that everyone shares it. In fact, it is more comfortable talking about its vision than many other types of organizations are. Just as some ST organizations are driven by their picture of how things were and are, the ENFJ organization is drawn forward by some picture of how things could be or even will be in the future.

The ENFJ organization is characterized by a high degree of human interaction. Cooperation is expected and human issues are espoused, although the actions of the organization may often fall short of its ideals. Because human needs are taken so seriously, this kind of organization frequently has an undercurrent of conflict and turbulence beneath the cooperative surface. Cooperation and conflict are the two sides of the same people-are-important coin.

ENFJ organizations are very interested in organizational cultures and take them seriously. Values are cherished by ENFJ organizations, and ideas or principles may take a back seat. Communications, whatever their overt content, will probably also concern human issues or the human dimensions of nonhuman issues. Because they are addressed to the whole person, the communications of an ENFJ organization may well be less rationalistic and more symbolic than in other organizations.

The ENFJ style is proactive. It wants to make things happen and finds it hard to understand others whose style is to understand situations rather than to change them. The ENFJ organization usually spells out people's responsibilities clearly and expects that people will carry them out. But command is not the ENFJ style, so people are expected to be proactive in their efforts once their roles are agreed on.

ENFJ organizations have high goals, and they manage to live up to them surprisingly often. The other side of these goals is a sense of shortcoming, which may seldom be expressed but is often just under the surface—a feeling of being less than it should be. No matter how successful it is, the ENFJ organization is likely to push for more. Unfortunately, this push can lead to unrealistic expectations and a general feeling of being overwhelmed with the possibilities and the needs of the situation.

This tendency toward overreaching is made more difficult because the ENFJ organization may not fully develop its systems—its formal procedures, financial controls, general policies, personnel regulations, management structures, and the like. Depending on people—not on their roles, but on their talents and integrity—ENFJ organizations have a tendency to look down on and underestimate the importance of rules and standards. This can hurt the organization, especially if and when it grows large.

The leadership of the ENFJ organization is often focused in a charismatic individual, although it may also be diffused among a tightly knit team. In either case, there is a strong democratic strand in the organizational value system. There is much talk of teamwork and a distrust of fixed hierarchies. Leaders in such organizations are likely to operate somewhat intuitively and with the kinds of mixed results (great successes and significant miscues) that intuitive leadership is prone to.

Leaders usually manage their public relations pretty well and spend a good deal of time communicating with their various constituencies. The negative aspect of the characteristic is that the vision being espoused sometimes slips over into hype and loses touch with the hard-edged aspects of reality.

The ENFJ organization handles unstructured or ambiguous situations better than many types of organizations do, though it can sometimes get into difficulty because of its natural tendency to wing it when a more carefully thought-out approach would be better. It can also emphasize *significance* to the detriment of *fact*: What things mean is much more interesting than what they are. This can result in a sort of idealism that can undermine the organization's sense of reality and can also contribute to the tendency toward hype.

The ENFJ organization can usually depend on high levels of commitment from people, although if it is not careful, those commitments can be overstretched and can lead to burnout. It is hard for ENFJ organizations *not* to tackle something if it obviously needs to be done— especially if the needs are human ones.

Herman Miller, the well-known furniture maker, would probably be an ENFJ organization. So is Nordstrom's, which has dominated its market with what can only be called organizational charisma, but which has also recently come in for criticism because of the very high expectations under which its salespeople work.

The ENFP Organization

Extraverted—focuses outward, responds to external stimuli
Intuitive—concerns itself with possibilities, attends to the big picture
Feeling—reaches conclusions on the basis of values and beliefs
Perceiving—likes to keep options open, distrusts too much definition

ENFP organizations tend to fall into two categories: the creative organization that develops new ideas or products for people, and the idealistic organization that focuses on developing, serving, or enlightening people. In either case, such organizations see the possibilities in and for people.

The ENFP organization can have difficulty with the aspects of its tasks that involve structures and systems. It wants to believe that people are basically good and that if trusted and encouraged they will do the right thing. ENFP organizations contrast themselves with organizations that lack heart, that have narrow beliefs, and that try to control people with rules. But those more "rigid" organizations often have an advantage when the environment or the internal situation gets more complex than goodwill and deep concern can handle.

Leaders in ENFP organizations try to resist issuing orders and mandates. They try to persuade, often by appeals to common values, and are usually willing to reconsider plans on the basis of subsequent input. They tend to be reactive and, in spite of their sensitivity to external signals, will sometimes stick with a once-promising situation much longer than they should. This can lead to trouble when a strong, proactive initiative is necessary to reverse direction.

ENFP organizations also have some difficulty with detail and follow-through. They see the possibility and they get the vision, but then they expect that things will unfold satisfactorily according to some natural pattern. (They also prefer oral communication to written communication, which sometimes makes it hard to keep track of agreements and decisions.) If they are not controlled, these tendencies can lead to a history of tackling projects with great enthusiasm—which ENFP organizations are good at generating with their employees or their clients—making promising beginnings, then losing interest and drifting off into other projects, which they undertake with the same excitement and hope as the last ones.

ENFP organizations are usually interesting, exciting places to work. They are often innovative and not afraid to experiment, so new things are always happening. They tend to be egalitarian: Everyone has a voice and perhaps even a vote. No one feels left out, although such inclusion takes a long time and may even come to be treated as a sort of end in itself. In that case, consensus is achieved at the expense of production.

People who gravitate to ENFP organizations are optimistic and likely to see the best in one another. But there is a shadow side to all this: Painful, confusing, or difficult things may be discounted and swept under the rug. In the name of getting along together, people may avoid problems that are thus left to grow unchecked until a crisis point. In this case, the ENFP organization can become the opposite of its optimistic and trusting self, turning instead into a bitter and paranoid operation that acts as though it has been victimized and hunts out the traitor or the culprit.

ENFP organizations are sensitive to subtle signals in their environments, so they are often the first to pick up cues about trends and emerging possibilities. In their fields they are often seen as cutting-edge organizations. But this tendency, too, has its darker side. Trend-spotting can degenerate into trendiness. Worse, their intuitive impression of the environment, while sensitive, can also be just plain wrong. ENFP organizations don't think much of hard data, so they aren't likely to test their impressions logically or systematically. Thus they can find themselves lost in exciting wild-goose chases and can be hurt in the process.

Internally, the ENFP organization expects harmony. It provides people with a lot of room to do their own thing, although it expects those separate efforts to add up to a collective purpose. It is sociable and democratic, an easy place to be. Without detailed standard operating procedures to follow, it is a good place for people who like freedom, although it is not so good for people who need supervision.

In handling change, it has the advantage of spotting the trend early and being able to reorient itself to the emerging reality rather easily. But the danger is that this reorientation process may be followed by another (as another trend is spotted) and yet another. Without much interest in formalizing procedures and policies and without much concern for precisely defined roles, the ENFP organization runs the danger of becoming so fluid that it is always on the verge of dissolving.

Because of their characteristics, many ENFP organizations do not last long enough or grow big enough to be widely known. One that has done so is W. L. Gore & Associates, the developers and manufacturers of Gore-Tex fabric, which has grown and thrived without any titles or hierarchy. Within a corporation, the public relations department may be ENFP, and some marketing departments share this character as well.

The ENTP Organization

Extraverted—focuses outward, responds to external stimuli
Intuitive—concerns itself with possibilities, attends to the big picture
Thinking—depends on impersonal procedures and principles
Perceiving—likes to keep options open, distrusts too much definition

The ENTP organization is an upbeat, can-do organization that is at its best designing or inventing an answer to a difficult problem. Because difficulties are likely to stimulate rather than discourage creativity, it will tackle projects that other organizations might dismiss, doing so as much because they are interesting than because of any practical gain. To say that something cannot be done is a challenge to ENTP organizations. Their love of conceptualizing and solving problems can turn work into a kind of game.

The negative side of this strength is that the game may lose its excitement once the problem is solved—even if the solution is still only on paper or in someone's head. All the hard work of turning the answer into a practical product or implementing a complex change is likely to seem a bit boring to the ENTP organization. Hence, it may move on to a new problem and fail to benefit materially from its insight and creativity in dealing with the old one.

If the organization is in a business that pays well for this early stage of doing things, it can do well. But if it is in a business where widgets have to be produced in quantity or a service has to be standardized so as to be done by fairly unskilled people, the ENTP organization is neither so interested nor so effective. At its best, such an organization may make important discoveries and creations. At its worst, it has a series of promising beginnings that never materialize into profitable ventures.

The ENTP impulse lends itself to the idea of continuous improvement, since every new situation is a problem to be solved and there is no need to stop and operate with the outcome of any previous problem-solving effort. This approach capitalizes on improvisation, and it improvises both internally and externally. As a result, it is good at adapting to changing situations— even to several different changes that are going on at once. But it may also become enamored of change and forget that one needs to slow down and develop a system to produce lasting results.

These organizations are seldom solidly hierarchical. Leadership is often more a matter of intelligence and creativity than position, and the result is that the leaders do not really have followers but simply colleagues or associates. The inventor genius may be a hero in this organization, but such a person probably lacks organizational ability and may actually be a very poor leader.

The ENTP organization tends to value quickness. Anyone who functions slowly or deliberately will get left by the wayside; the organization is intolerant of people who need things explained several times or who take a while to get used to a new situation. Nor is it tolerant of people with high security needs. On the contrary, it is drawn to problematic and, therefore, risky situations. People who like such situations feel at home there, and people who don't, do not.

ENTP organizations like debate. They do not push for closure very quickly, viewing positively the process of discussion and inquiry. Nor are they sensitive to people who get hurt in the rough give and take of debate. You are supposed to be able to hold your own in this game of criticism and challenge. You are supposed to get the picture quickly and start developing it or refining it or translating it. To be slow and deliberate is not to fit in, although ironically this type of organization usually needs such people as a corrective to its own mercurial tendencies.

The ENTP organization does not take formal procedures or practical regulations very seriously. Even *reality* is treated as only one variable in the situation—a variable that is subject to creative reshaping. Combined with the ENTP tendency to do more than one thing at a time, this can mean that the organization's practical affairs are often a mess. That may not be a serious problem when the organization is small, but if it grows, the ENTP organization may well face a crisis when its own workings become too complex to be conducted in its favored seat-of-the-pants fashion.

ENTP organizations are found in the fields of research and development—either as stand-alone companies or as departments of a corporation. A consulting business may prosper if it has this style. Start-up companies, too, may do well, at least for a while, since the early phases of the start-up process may involve demonstrating that something can be done rather than doing it over and over again. Xerox's famous Palo Alto Research Center is an example that has lasted and is still vital, but many others pass through this phase and either grow beyond it or fail to survive. Atari is a classic case of the latter sort.

The ESTP Organization

Extraverted—focuses outward, responds to external stimuli
Sensing—concerns itself with actualities, attends to details
Thinking—depends on impersonal procedures and principles
Perceiving—likes to keep options open, distrusts too much definition

Whatever its formal business, the ESTP organization is likely to have a somewhat entrepreneurial style. It is resourceful, able to capitalize on turns of events that it did not necessarily foresee but is still able to turn to its benefit in ways that other types of organizations find difficult. This is partly because ESTP organizations do not identify very closely with the past and partly because the SP combination means that they don't find much satisfaction in developing the kinds of formal procedures and policies that are natural barriers to change.

The ESTP organization thrives on its ability to manipulate the external environment in some way. It is good at doing that, in part, because it instinctively views its environment as a situation full of unmet needs and problems to be solved. Actions, not ideas, are what count. There is a verve and vitality about ESTP action that is exciting to watch.

The organization is good at quick, pragmatic analyses of situations. It is not hampered by inner rules or frightened of any risk that can be rationally assessed. So ESTP organizations sometimes act as if they were engaged in an adventure and have nothing to lose. This tendency is useful in crisis or high-risk situations where other organizations are more hesitant, although it can also make them grow bored when things calm down. Then they may either go inert for a while or else stir up a new crisis to deal with.

Sometimes they seem to stir up crises internally, too. They thrive on frequent change—even if some of their employees do not—and so they reorganize to meet this situation and then reorganize again to meet that one. Moving fast, they can be unreliable on their commitments growing from past situations. They also tend not to be very concerned with the kind of detailed follow-through that is necessary to turn a quick fix into a long-term solution. But given a situation that requires their strengths, they can accomplish what few organizations can.

Relatively uninterested in inner human motivations, the ESTP approach is not very empathic or cognizant of subtle human issues. Its analyses can be flawed by the absence of important factors that are not logical. The same disinterest leads to an underestimation of the diverse motivations of its own employees, so that when the crisis passes, it may find itself with dissatisfaction on its hands at home.

The ESTP organization prefers to focus on the present and forget the past, which is (by its way of thinking) done with, gone, finished. Nor is it very concerned with planning for the future. For those reasons, the ESTP organization may have trouble sustaining long efforts and learning from its mistakes. It can go from great success to catastrophe quickly. But its pragmatism keeps it from becoming wedded to any one way of doing things, so it can also bounce back from difficulty quickly and sometimes even transform catastrophe into success.

The preference for shooting from the hip also discourages the establishment of formal procedures. The tendency toward ad hoc solutions can create inconsistency. The impersonal focus on the situation can lead to emotional issues being swept under the rug, and the same focus can lead to an abrasive and impatient management style that carries within it the seeds of its own destruction. The competitive thrust that can win a particular contract or battle can also alienate people or create a negative public image with other potential clients.

For better and worse, the ESTP organization is the archetypal hustler, the firefighter, the gunslinger organization that subdues disorder and then moves on. Motivated largely by pleasure in its own action, it has little time to muse over the more distant future or even to worry about what to do after the immediate fire is put out. It needs new fires, and as long as they occur and as long as it can keep a work force motivated to put them out, the organization can be very successful. But by its nature, it is not concerned about becoming a long-lived organization.

Red Adair's company of oil well firefighters are quintessentially ESTP. So are many start-up businesses outside the high-tech area. Such businesses usually don't grow very old or large. But occasionally one does, or else it recovers this spirit in a drive to become entrepreneurial and more risk taking. One such organization is Citibank.

The ESFP Organization

Extraverted—focuses outward, responds to external stimuli
Sensing—concerns itself with actualities, attends to details
Feeling—reaches conclusions on the basis of values and beliefs
Perceiving—likes to keep options open, distrusts too much definition

The ESFP organization lives by giving clients and customers exactly what they want. The outcome may be a product or service, but no other type of organization is as good at sensing the hungers and tastes of the public and satisfying them. It would not be too much to say that the ESFP organization views almost anything it does as a form of entertainment, fast food, or quick service. Everything that is done involves a transaction in which a client's desire for diversion, novelty, or engagement is satisfied immediately—at least for the moment. Whether the output is an experience or an object, the ESFP organization deals best with things that are consumed in the here and now.

This kind of organization can also provide its own people with pleasant experiences and material benefits. These organizations are likely to treat work as a kind of play-for-pay and to assume that people get their pleasure as much from the doing as from the formal reward it brings. There is likely to be a sense of fun about what is done, and there may be a friendly kind of competition among co-workers, as there would be on a sports team. A note of spontaneity runs through the activity, and even routine assignments are carried out as though there were a spur-of-the-moment quality to them.

The ESFP organization is pragmatic and unconcerned with precedent or formal procedure. This does not necessarily mean that it is efficient—that might require too much structure or too much planning. But where skill, enthusiasm, and energy can carry the day, the ESFP organization will shine.

It has little tolerance for anxiety or stress, and interpersonal tension is denied as long as possible. The result is that real problems can build up until they are dangerously large. Similarly, since there is little interest in long-range plans, emerging changes in the external world are likely to arrive on the organization's doorstep without much warning. ESFP organizations may, given their skill at improvisation, deal effectively with such issues spontaneously. But then again, the problems may be too big or complex to be handled that way.

It is ironic that this kind of organization, which is so preoccupied with giving people what they want, should be so poor at foreseeing what they are *going to* want. It is similarly poor at foreseeing some of the impact of its actions on its own people, and so is as likely to be surprised by internal as by external developments.

ESFP organizations tend to be good at public relations and at maintaining a good image in the public eye because they are good at understanding how the public wants to see them. But making an actual change that would transform how the organization really *is* is difficult for ESFP organizations. As a result, their changes are often cosmetic and meant simply to placate external groups, rather than growing out of the organization's actual needs.

ESFP organizations are a little like tops. As long as they are spinning fast, they stay up. But when they slow down, they are heading for trouble. This gives many of them a frenetic quality, as though they didn't dare to pause to take stock and see how they are doing. And it also makes them both changeworthy and change phobic. They can switch fast by picking up cues accurately and acting accordingly. But they may not see nor respond to the big changes coming farther down the track.

Consequently, they may not have very long lives. In some businesses, where it is particularly important to ride the wave of fashion and opinion in the short run, they can be quite successful. If they can build a unique management system that fits their character, they can also grow and thrive—as Mary Kay Cosmetics has done.

The ISTJ Organization

Introverted—takes cues and draws power from within, is fairly closed
Sensing—concerns itself with actualities, attends to details
Thinking—depends on impersonal procedures and principles
Judging—likes things spelled out and definite, seeks closure

The ISTJ is the stablest of organizations, although when hit by a big, unexpected change it can be knocked for a loop. The basic stability and reliability of the organization's functional systems—which it creates and protects quite un–self-consciously—is magnified by the fact that the organization is likely to be rather closed to outsiders. Thus, its internal processes are not very evident to the external world, which contributes to its image as an organization that has it all together. The same closed quality, however, may make it difficult for anyone but an insider to spot internal problems early. Therefore, problems occasionally get out of hand before they are acknowledged.

The spirit of the organization is likely to be efficient and low-key. Down deep, the ISTJ organization considers it in bad taste to brag or toot its own horn. For that reason, its power is sometimes underestimated by those not in the know. ISTJ organizations move rather slowly and deliberately and seldom enter a new situation without careful thought. Therefore, they don't often make blunders or build up expectations that they cannot fulfill. They don't amaze, but they don't disappoint either. Their word is their bond.

They focus on turning out their own services or products, and under decent circumstances they do this very well. They live by schedules and meet their deadlines. People in them are expected to work hard, and people drawn to them usually do. There is no type of organization that is so reliable when it comes to getting all the details right. If the organization is involved in financial matters, it is likely to focus on the preservation of capital rather than the generation of large incomes. And this same spirit governs ISTJ conduct when it comes to nonfinancial materials as well. It takes care of things and sees to it that they aren't lost or damaged.

ISTJ organizations subdue disorder wherever they find it, and they protect against disorder when they cannot subdue it. They guard, they nurture, they insure, they shelter—and they inspect to see that they are doing it right. Because of their protective tendency, they are often drawn to efforts that involve the preservation of community "capital" in the form of human resources or historical heritage or traditional knowledge. In so doing, they form the keel of the community ship, keeping it on course and discouraging drift.

By the same token, they discourage rapid change and don't take chances very comfortably. They may, therefore, lose contact with their market if it changes quickly, and they don't really belong in markets that do. Even in less rapidly changing situations, they can lock on to a once-productive way of doing things and lose out on changes that could actually benefit them.

ISTJ organizations are at their best when they have a plan to implement or a clear design to follow. They do less well coming up with that initial design. It is not that they do not have ideas and plans. It is simply that how things are done is so important to them that they are on their own home field when the time comes to carry out any undertaking.

ISTJ organizations tend to distrust theory or brilliance; they put their money on hard work. They respect experience and tend to assume that hierarchy embodies it and should be honored. Their values are not marginal or unusual—they are mainstream. They are clear about what they believe and may preach it to others. They can even become intolerant and dogmatic.

Logic and good sense appeal to them. Intuition and radical innovations make them nervous. They tend to prefer written documents and distrust oral communication. They are likely to have generated and preserved little rituals, often harking back to the organization's origin.

Internally, ISTJ organizations are likely to be organized functionally and to provide people with clear expectations and role responsibilities. In big organizations, this tendency can produce a collection of somewhat isolated domains between which communication is difficult. To get ahead is to contribute to one of these functional domains. Credentials are important, and so is experience. ISTJ cultures are conventional, and they may develop an us-versus-them polarity with whatever is unconventional. But those who qualify as *us* get a powerful sense of belonging from being part of an ISTJ organization and feel great loyalty toward it.

The traditional old-line corporation that does things logically and follows time-tested ways is likely to be an ISTJ. That type dominated the steel industry, the telephone business, the utility industry, and the world of most public bureaucracies for decades. Sears and GM are both ISTJ, though like most such organizations, they are currently trying to become more E and N—though not F or P. Inside any company or institution, finance and administration are very likely to be ISTJ departments.

The ISFJ Organization

Introverted—takes cues and draws power from within, is fairly closed
Sensing—concerns itself with actualities, attends to details
Feeling—reaches conclusions on the basis of values and beliefs
Judging—likes things spelled out and definite, seeks closure

The ISFJ organization is at its best when it is doing something where hard work and responsibility count for a lot, especially if it can be supported by the lessons of the past. It takes human issues seriously, so it does not apply its experience mechanically or impersonally. For the same reason, it is fairly responsive to the needs and concerns of its client.

But it is responsive within a context of tradition—it does not get caught up in trendiness. Over time, ISFJ organizations develop a way of doing things that is comfortable and that even gains a bit of a ritual quality. "At X, we do it this way." Why? Because that's a tried and true way to do it—and because the world is a difficult and even dangerous place. For every gain the organization may make in experimenting, it also leaves itself open to loss. "Win some, lose some" is not reassuring to the ISFJ organization.

This traditionalism may express itself externally in mottoes and little ceremonies that may seem silly to outsiders, but which are cherished by all but the newest employees and clients. Even the newest people in the ISFJ community get attention, for this type of organization is good at bringing along new people and making them part of the group. Not surprisingly, people get a sense of belonging from an ISFJ organization.

They also get a sense of solidity. The ISFJ organization acts as though it'll always be around. No brief candles or overnight sensations. The organization takes care of its people, and it will take care of you if you are one of *us*. The negative side is that there is a kind of emotional stock-taking going on within the organization. Although a newcomer may not understand it until too late, there is an invisible credit-and-debit sheet that tracks what you have contributed and what the organization has done for you. People who aren't used to such a system find that they have run up some kind of mysterious debt in people's eyes: They seem to owe the company something. And in time, that can become oppressive.

Back on the positive side, the ISFJ solidity comes from a reliability that has been codified into standard operating procedures. (It may, in fact, be easier to understand the rules than the roles, because sometimes responsibilities are less clearly defined than procedures.) There may be handbooks to cover all the issues that might come up, and if there aren't, you can usually find the right answer from someone who has worked there for a while. The answer will always be a sensible one, too.

The no-nonsense quality to the ISFJ organization quiets many doubts. The leaders aren't chasing rainbows, and the investments are in blue-chip securities. Everyone exercises economic responsibility. The products may not be fancy or state-of-the-art, but they work, and the organization will stand behind them. Even if the organization conducts a competitive business, there is a kind of service-to-others quality about it. This comes out all the more strongly when the organization is in a service field.

The difficulty that an ISFJ organization can get into comes when its admirable perseverance and dedication is to the wrong or the out-of-date thing. Then there is trouble. The leadership of the typical ISFJ organization isn't very concerned with spotting change in advance, so they sometimes need to collide with it before they take it seriously and begin to respond.

The difficulty is not over then, for the ISFJ organization, with its solid hierarchy and its standard operating procedures, is not a very flexible organization. Reorganization is traumatic, and technological change can lead to great distress. Only when such changes can be done in small steps is the organization comfortable with them. As a result, ISFJ organizations believe in the incremental theory of progress and mistrust big transformative projects.

Because decision making is likely to be kept relatively private in this type of organization, employees cannot readily see what is going on. They are supposed to trust their superiors, and things go well as long as they do. But if that trust starts to break down, the ISFJ organization is in real trouble—more than some other organizations where trust and consensus and belonging are not so important.

If trouble does occur, there will be talk about the good old days and how the present leadership overreacted. People will say that the organization is falling apart, and in the end the ISFJ organization can be crippled by a change that a more flexible organization could have managed without great difficulty.

ISFJ organizations have many similarities to ISTJ organizations, although they are more likely to engage in human activities. For this reason, many hospitals and schools fall into this category. So do insurance companies like Metropolitan Life and Aetna. In their diversification ventures during the eighties, they tried to become more E and N. Time will tell whether they succeeded or whether their fundamental character got in the way of their uncharacteristic activities.

The INTJ Organization

Introverted—takes cues and draws power from within, is fairly closed
Intuitive—concerns itself with possibilities, attends to the big picture
Thinking—depends on impersonal procedures and principles
Judging—likes things spelled out and definite, seeks closure

The INTJ organization is independent, innovative, iconoclastic, and likely to regard itself as unique. Often focused on intellectual or scientific ventures, INTJ organizations are best at developing some essential idea into a service or a product, or else applying an existing idea to some entirely new area. Forceful and undeterred by conventional objections, they make decisions fairly quickly and accurately. They dislike inefficiency and will never settle for something because it has always been done that way.

The voice of authority means little if they see what they believe to be the truth or the reality. They are pragmatic: Everything demands proof, everything is up for discussion. There are no sacred cows. INTJ organizations are often pioneers in their fields, blazing the way that other less confident organizations will follow. They can see opportunities when other organizations claim that all the opportunities are gone, and they often discover possibilities, particularly of a practical or technological nature, when other organizations dismiss a situation as unpromising or even hopeless.

The INTJ forte is strategy, however, not tactics. Often the creative solution is more interesting to the organization than the detailed plan of turning it into a viable product. There is more interest in understanding things than in making things. And there is even a tendency for the organization to want things to conform to the intellectual model rather than accepting things as they are. So the INTJ organization's results sometimes fall short of the expectations people have for them.

The INTJ organization has another serious failing. It is likely to be insensitive to the human aspects of whatever it is doing. This may mean that it underestimates the external distress caused by its actions and that employee reactions are unforeseen. The organization is likely to expect employees to subordinate personal concerns and see the logic of the situation. When people react to its actions with strong feeling, it always complains that they are over reacting.

The INTJ organization is fairly impervious to criticism. It is hard for outsiders to get much of an idea about how it functions, which mutes criticism by hiding what is going on. But it also generates criticism among people who are suspicious of what they cannot see. The self-confidence with which the organization steers its own course can turn into stubbornness, and if the organization gets off on the wrong track somehow, that stubbornness can be disastrous—because INTJ organizations do not easily admit that they have been wrong. They succeed by willpower, and they fail by willpower.

They are internally flexible. They expect their employees to be able to shift work groups readily and to handle multiple or ambiguous reporting relationships. They also expect them to understand what is expected of them quickly, and if things must be explained more than once or if a training program does not generate results quickly, there is likely to be impatience. In INTJ organizations, people are supposed to "get the idea" and not need much detailed direction.

These organizations are at their best in situations where there are possibilities in a new situation to be capitalized on. They will then make whatever changes are called for and reorganize to meet the challenge. Other organizations often seem sluggish and timid by comparison.

They are in more trouble, however, with changes that are forced on them. To be able to choose one's challenge is important to them, and INTJ organizations do not take kindly to pressure. When it is the organization's own inner workings that are the problem, the INTJ organization is in even more trouble and can quickly lose momentum and go into a dangerous period of confusion.

INTJ organizations are often creative, although the creativity is usually more intellectual than artistic. Rational innovation is their strength. They operate fast—fast analysis, fast solution. But people often feel rushed by their speed. They are impatient with ritual, viewing it as something close to hocus-pocus. They like to deal with information and are impatient with the softer relational side of communication, which they dismiss as touchy-feely or small talk. So they don't handle their human relations very well, forgetting that people need appreciation and that there is a wisdom of the heart as well as of the head.

Viewing people as essentially elements in a system, they have a rather narrow concept of support and motivation. This can work for highly technical researchers, but it doesn't work so well for other kinds of employees, who often feel that they have been forgotten and taken for granted.

At their best, such companies are very creative: AT&T's Bell Labs are a famous and very successful example. At their worst, they are simply demanding places with very little heart.

The INFJ Organization

Introverted—takes cues and draws power from within, is fairly closed
Intuitive—concerns itself with possibilities, attends to the big picture
Feeling—reaches conclusions on the basis of values and beliefs
Judging—likes things spelled out and definite, seeks closure

The INFJ organization operates quietly, but behind the scenes there is a powerful commitment to the goals and values that the organization espouses. The goals are value driven, so that whatever field the organization is in, its beliefs are what define its purpose and strategy. If these beliefs are ever lost or compromised, the organization is in trouble.

Most INFJ organizations take their people seriously, although one might not realize at first glance that people are so important. The external appearance of the organization is straightforward and somewhat matter-of-fact, and one can easily underestimate the organization's power, imagination, and passion because of the aura of responsibility the organization conveys.

This type of organization is actually rather creative, although it may not make very much of the fact. Some of its decisions are made and ventures initiated with a kind of a sixth sense for the possibilities of the situation. (Again, this may not be recognizable until one is inside the organization.)

This makes its processes a little mysterious, so outsiders are unlikely to find it easy to know what is going on inside the INFJ organization.

The leadership will reflect these values: capable, intuitive, responsible, modest, and driven by deeply felt values. The leadership is likely to be adaptable and responsive to changing situations—at least until one of its basic values is threatened in some way. Then the leadership, and perhaps the whole organization, will dig in with a stubbornness that can surprise an outsider.

Under the surface (which can be a fairly conventional one), there is probably a good deal of human interaction going on. Conflict is avoided as much as possible, and much time and energy goes into working through internal stresses. Staff harmony is sought and expected.

Internally and externally, there is likely to be sensitivity to criticism, even when that criticism is relatively minor or obviously misdirected. But the positive side of this sensitivity is an awareness of the customer or the client and the real needs the organization is seeking to meet. The organization may even be in the business of acting as an advocate for those needs.

Personnel policies tend to emphasize using people's individual capabilities. Plans must withstand the test of general benefit. But INFJ organizations also tend to presume fairly heavy commitments from people. This makes the INFJ organization both a comfortable place to work (because you can be yourself) and a demanding one (because you'd better care). If the high expectations aren't monitored, they can lead to burnout—especially because people attracted to these organizations already have high expectations of themselves.

One way that INFJ organizations can deal with this tendency toward burnout is through communal events and ceremonies, for these fit the INFJ style well. There is an imaginative and even symbolic streak in the INFJ organization that can lead to impressive ceremonies. Developmental activities of all kinds fit the INFJ style as well: training, mentoring and coaching, and career planning. So if the organization runs the risk of burning people out, it also has resources for dealing with the problem.

INFJ organizations handle change pretty well—if the change fits in with their values. But crises and radical reversals of expectations are difficult. With their emphasis on discussion and bringing everyone on board whatever is done, INFJ organizations can weather severe storms. Johnson & Johnson's handling of the Tylenol poisoning is such a case. But they can also move fairly slowly and run into difficulties for that reason. They can spend so much time getting everyone involved that the time for opportune action can be missed.

The INFP Organization

Introverted—takes cues and draws power from within, is fairly closed
Intuitive—concerns itself with possibilities, attends to the big picture
Feeling—reaches conclusions on the basis of values and beliefs
Perceiving—likes to keep options open, distrusts too much definition

---

The INFP organization is likely to be on a crusade of some kind—either overtly or covertly. This may not be a social crusade, but rather a quest for a better technique, a better product, or a better service. The motivation here is not competitive. It is idealistic—the dream of helping, improving, fixing, saving. Behind most INFP organizations is some basic dream to improve individual lives or the world.

This fact may not be obvious to outsiders, since the INFP organization tends to be private in its workings. Its values are powerful, but they may not be articulated very fully or expressed very often to the external world. This is an organization that really cares, but that fact may be clearer inside its walls than outside.

In many ways, the INFP organization is likely to have a youthful feeling about it. It may not be a new organization in years, but it has a quality of optimism and hopefulness that is the very opposite of world-weary or timeworn. This can make the organization a little naive and can weaken its chances of success in the marketplace. The other weakness that has the same effect is its distaste for formal business procedures and organizational systems. The INFP organization may have a chart showing whom everyone reports to, but things don't always work the way they do on paper. This type of organization will always have difficulty with tasks that require solid structures and systems, and anyone who tries to build them may be treated as uptight, too rationalistic, and someone who lacks faith in people.

The INFP organization operates on the assumption that people mean well and that when things go wrong it is because of oversights or misunderstandings. For that reason, they have difficulty with people or organizations that do not have their best interests at heart. The INFP organization turns such difficulty into a virtue—the virtue of trust—and embodies it in a whole psychological theory about the benefits of positive reinforcement and how people will live up to the image you have of them. This half-truth takes them a long way, but it often puts them at a disadvantage when they are competing with organizations that take a darker view of human nature.

There aren't many standard operating procedures to keep things happening in a predictable way. Individual needs and the opportunities of the moment usually dictate how things will be done. This may make it hard for new people in the organization to learn how to do things, and it may make the results inconsistent. When the organization is small—as many INFP organizations are—this will not be a problem. (It will probably, in fact, be a source of pride.) But as the organization gets larger or more complex or as it tries to do more complex things, this lack of systems is going to be a problem.

In handling change, the INFP organization is at its best in sensing the potentials of situations, especially human situations. This gives it an early cue as to trends and makes it possible to launch changes effectively. Its weaker suit is in follow-through, and the tendency is for promising beginnings to die on the vine when the systematic tasks of implementation are called for.

But the INFP organization is adaptable, and so it is not likely to be long at a loss for a new cause or new endeavor. And with its tendency to do things in an aesthetically pleasing way, the INFP organization can sometimes flow from one focus to another in ways that would pull another kind of organization apart.

Some social reform and environmental advocacy groups fall into this category. In its early days, Apple Computer would have also, with its emphasis on empowering the individual and changing the world through computing. So would many young ventures that are never heard from again. It's a tough organization to keep alive over time, and many INFP companies grow more S, T, and J with time. But it's certainly a fascinating kind of organization while it is around.

The INTP Organization

Introverted—takes cues and draws power from within, is fairly closed
Intuitive—concerns itself with possibilities, attends to the big picture
Thinking—depends on impersonal procedures and principles
Perceiving—likes to keep options open, distrusts too much definition

The INTP organization is at its best dealing with systems and designs, but its focus is on understanding or creating them and not on implementing them or building them into replicable products. It does not engage in activities that require it to do things over and over again in a routine way. It can hang in with a problem for a long time and hold a consistent effort to the task of solving it, for it is not easily discouraged. But when the problem has been solved, attention is likely to move on to the next problem rather than following through on the discovery.

The organization is attuned to whatever is emerging in the world. Since it is also one of the most creative of organizational types, it often finds itself on the cutting edge of its field. Its efforts are most stimulated by difficulty and complexity. "It can't be done" is a challenge. Objections that involve "reality" are dismissed as simply conventional thinking. Rules are usually treated as little more than conventional techniques or trivial technicalities.

From the outside, INTP organizations are often rather mysterious. This is partly because they tend to operate in a somewhat intuitive way and to follow hunches that are hard to explain logically. But it is also because they are private organizations that don't feel any need to justify themselves to outsiders. For these reasons, INTP organizations tend to be loners in the organizational world. They go their own way, don't communicate very well with other organizations, and don't join in associations or joint ventures the way more open, interactional organizations do. They may not even communicate very well to their clients, viewing them almost as unfortunate necessities rather than as the underpinning of their business.

The intuitive strength of this kind of organization can also be its downfall. Not only does it make the organization relatively uninterested in practical application, but it can also lead it to chase rainbows if it locks onto a brilliant idea that proves to be unworkable. It can also pursue directions that seriously trouble or even harm its employees, for it is relatively unaware of and uninterested in their feelings. Feeling is dismissed as merely personal and is of a much lower order than ideas, which are important and impersonal. Needless to say, many employees find this attitude difficult, so INTP organizations tend to keep only employees who can live with this way of doing things.

The leadership of the INTP organization is likely to find these values acceptable and to expect of others the kind of commitment which they themselves give to the organization. People are supposed to enjoy debate and not mind if they are criticized for fuzzy thinking or erroneous information. The leadership takes a lot for granted, of course, forgetting that they communicate poorly, make heavy demands on people, and expect the excitement of the process to be its own reward. With like-minded people, this can work. With folks of a different stripe, it leads to terrible morale.

The interpersonal relations within the INTP organization are somewhat distant, though not in the way they are in a hierarchical organization. In fact, there is a kind of egalitarianism among people here, so that good ideas are respected no matter who produces them. The one exception to the egalitarian spirit may be in relation to the founder, who is likely to be viewed as a genius and may be revered as larger than life.

INTP organizations are comfortable with change—if they dream it up and plan it. If it is forced on them, they may deny or denounce it—and resist it. There is a strong the-way-things-ought-to-be quality about their view of the world. If the world doesn't cooperate, so much the worse for the world!

They have difficulty with the human side of change—not too surprisingly. They also run into trouble whenever change demands that they build new systems to accomodate to it. There is a basic seat-of-the-pants approach to issues that is natural to INTP organizations as well as a resistance to formalizing things. This works best when organizations are small or simple and works less and less well if they grow and become complex.

Many INTP organizations are part of something bigger—a venture capital group at a larger firm or a product development group at a large corporation. Or they are small and new, with a very uncertain future. One that "grew up" is Polaroid, which hit a home run with its great photographic innovation, but it has lacked the EJ character that stays in touch with what the market wants or what internal management systems demand. Instead, it developed products, like instant movie film, that no one really wanted. It also found it hard to keep its momentum up after the departure of its founder, Edwin H. Land.

The ISTP Organization

Introverted—takes cues and draws power from within, is fairly closed
Sensing—concerns itself with actualities, attends to details
Thinking—depends on impersonal procedures and principles
Perceiving—likes to keep options open, distrusts too much definition

The ISTP organization tends to be fairly egalitarian, distrusting hierarchy and formal authorities. Its culture emphasizes, as much as its situation permits, "doing your own thing." There will be a spontaneous quality about the organization and its actions, and it may have a sort of quixotic tendency to tilt against the odds. There is something adventurous that one feels in many ISTP organizations—an enjoyment of the action, a willingness to take risks, and even a little impulsiveness.

Unlike many others, the ISTP organization would not at all like to run the world. Their goal is more modest: to do some one thing well and to get pleasure out of doing it. What that thing is will vary, but it is usually based on some kind of mastery of a process, an art, or some kind of equipment. The satisfaction provided by the ISTP organization is that of being able to do the thing it is good at for people who want and need it done—to do it well and to be recognized for its accomplishment. The virtuosi of various practices are to be found in these organizations, and the spirit of excellence and excitement that they generate are likely to be evident.

The organization as such exists to make this activity possible. It may be fairly primitive in the management sense, and its leadership may exist mainly to make the masters' work possible. There won't be much concern about communication, and so complex coordination or planning efforts are difficult. Regulations and policies are likely to be sketchy, and those that exist will always be bent to fit the situation. Since talent is prized, training is likely to be rather undervalued.

There is a performance quality about the services or products that the organization offers: They are provided for their effect, the experience they afford, or their entertainment value. Quality may be emphasized, but it will be as much for its aesthetic value as for its functional quality. Efficiency may be prized, but it will be an efficiency of effort rather than a way of husbanding resources.

The organization itself is likely to be very simple, an adjunct to the actual contact with the customer, which is the moment that everything else—the records, the training, the management structure—is meant for. And in the end, nothing else matters very much, for essentially the organization is a bunch of independent performers under an organizational umbrella.

How does the ISTP handle change? It depends how the performers handle it. If they can respond to a changing audience demand, the organization will probably back them up. But the organization itself will not take the lead, will not plan, will not develop new resources, and will not market thoughtfully. So the organization has a kind of temporary quality about it.

Many new-product teams have this character, as do some start-up companies. So do some groups of craftspeople, performers, or athletes. There is little about the organization that resists change—so as long as its people can satisfy the public, the organization can survive.

The ISFP Organization

Introverted—takes cues and draws power from within, is fairly closed
Sensing—concerns itself with actualities, attends to details
Feeling—reaches conclusions on the basis of values and beliefs
Perceiving—likes to keep options open, distrusts too much definition

The ISFP organization is designed to make it possible for individual performers in some craft or art or profession to do what they do well. Hierarchy and authority in general are at best tolerated for the conditions of freedom that they create, and the result is often little islands of activity surrounded by a very loose network of support services.

The culture of the ISFP organization is individualistic and emphasizes expertise and grace. The organization's management structure hardly deserves its title, for it is little more than an umbrella under which the key individuals operate. Leadership similarly is minimal, unless it is embodied in a master performer or artisan, whom all the others admire.

This kind of organization depends for its continuity on countless little satisfactory encounters between the practitioners and their publics. If these practitioners are skillful and sensitive, they will stay in touch with those publics. But their own values may preclude changing what they do—which they would see as prostituting themselves—and so they may go out of favor. There is little long-range planning or formal marketing effort to keep that from happening.

Within the organization, there is little concern for formal communication. People may express themselves vocally, but there are seldom the concerted efforts that demand clear communication of intent and response to intent. The organization's records, training, and management structure are also informal. Formal systems are poorly developed and generally viewed as unnecessary.

The ways in which people interact within the ISFP organization have a pragmatic quality: "What are we doing this for? What do you want out of it? What do I want?" Individuals end up exerting more or less power depending on the particular situation and their own desires, so the pragmatism is efficient in only relatively uncomplicated situations.

The work itself has a peculiar quality to it: It is more a form of play or a game or a contest than it is work in the conventional sense. Skill, whatever its content, is esteemed, and competition is expected. The results of the competition may be a kind of ranking in excellence, but that does not translate into an organizational hierarchy any more than the seedings in a tennis tournament do. And as with such seedings, there is a colleagueship that cuts across the rankings.

The ways that ISFP organizations handle change depend on how the performers themselves handle it. They tend to like excitement and not to be afraid of risk, so there is nothing about change per se that frightens them. If they can continue to respond to a changing audience, the organization will probably back them up. But the organization itself will not take the lead, will not plan, will not develop new resources, and will not test-market. Yet it will not resist change either, for its positions do not constitute real power bases or turfs from which to view change as destructive.

All in all, the ISFP organization is a kind of anti-organization. It works best when it is part of some larger organization that can do for it what it cannot do for itself. If it is self-contained, one would not expect it to last very long. Rather, it would be more likely to die and be reborn as some similar organization—probably another ISFP. Some people spend their working lives going through this death and rebirth cycle with a sequence of ISFP organizations.

Chapter Four

Character, Growth, and Change

The Organizational Life Cycle

If it lasts long enough, any organization goes through a life cycle that begins with its conception and ends with its old age and death.[1] Unlike the individual life cycle, there is no life expectancy that we can assume for organizations. Many more organizations die in the very early phases of their lifetimes than is the case with individuals in any but those societies where chaos and scarcity make life very precarious. And a few organizations seem almost immortal. Such differences notwithstanding, it is useful to understand the basic stages of organizational growth and to focus some of the organization's developmental activity on helping the organization move from the stage that is passing to the next that is emerging.

To do that effectively, it is important to understand how character is affected by such life-cycle growth, as each phase of growth depends on the presence of some configuration of the types of organizational character we have been examining here. There are, for example, phases where the organization's introversion fits with what the phase demands and its extraversion does not. Extremely extraverted organizations have difficulty with such phases and may short-change them in such a way that a weakness is built into the organization at that point that proves problematic later on. In some cases, the difficulty is so great that the organization simply cannot accomplish the developmental task that lies at the heart of that phase. In that event, the organization either disintegrates or stagnates in a state of arrested development.

Phase One: The Dream

Every organization grows from some idea or image in someone's mind. Let's call it the *dream* of the organization. At this stage, nothing exists in the external world; it is pure potentiality. This is a time when there is not much actuality, only possibility. It is also a very fluid time, for the dream may be still unfolding and taking shape.[2] Whatever the natural character that organization will develop when it becomes manifest in the world, this phase has a characteristic shape of its own. It is introverted, intuitive, and perceiving: IN–P.[3]

An organization that is naturally extraverted, sensing, and judging may not have a very vital dream at its core, although there are long periods during the life cycle when that might not matter very much. As we shall see below, it will start to matter when the organization moves into its middle age and is in need of some kind of renewal. Since one way to renew an organization is either to recapture and redefine the original dream or to develop a new one, ES–J organizations are at a disadvantage when it comes to organizational self-renewal.

Phase Two: The Venture

At some point, the dream has to be realized in action if there is to be an organization. To bring the organization into existence in that sense takes extraversion and judging: the former because the essential dream has to come out into the world, and the latter because it has to take some definite form and identity. The characteristic shape of the venture, therefore, is E—J.

If the original I—P was too strong, it is likely to be one of those situations where "it was a great idea, but we could never quite get it off the drawing board." The world is full of such pipe dreams. If the original I—P is a little less strong, the organization may well come into being but be too weakly rooted in the real world to last. "We never attracted enough customers," they say, or, "We never quite figured out what we were—we tried to be all things to all people." The world is full of those false starts, too.

Phase Three: Getting Organized

The venture is a time of making it up as you go along, a time when hard work and commitment are critical. All you've got is a good idea and the willingness to put in long hours. If the idea is really good and you stick to it, the venture is likely to prosper and grow. Ventures can be barely a year old or can be ten years old, and under the right circumstances can become fairly large. (Apple became the first venture to make the Fortune 500 list.) But whatever their age and size, they are run without much structure or many policies. The management style is seat-of-the-pants. If something looks promising, you do it.

If they are successful, however, ventures grow to the point where they get too complicated for such looseness to work well. There are too many employees, too many customers, too much data, too much money, too many appointments, and so forth. It is going to be necessary to get organized, that is, to create systems and procedures to bring predictability to what was once just creative chaos.

Doing this requires the organization to refocus its attention inwardly (introversion) and to develop its sensing and thinking. So the characteristic shape of getting organized is IST–. Organizations weak in those aspects are going to carry forward a disorganized condition that will probably undermine their effectiveness and limit their growth if it does not in fact lead to their demise.

Phase Four: Making It

Barring an unusual catastrophe, a healthy venture that gets organized effectively is in a position to grow some more. But to establish itself fully as a force in its area of business requires entering a new developmental phase in which it really makes it. To do this, it must turn back outward again toward its market (extraversion), understand the emerging opportunities that are open to it (intuition), and establish bonds with both its own employees and its customers (feeling).

It can probably do with any two of these aspects. A powerful proprietary technology (introversion) can make it if it is aligned with opportunity (intuition) and backed by connections with people (feeling). Customer service (extraverted feeling) can sometimes carry the day without much intuition. And a powerful and innovative opportunism (extraverted intuition) can make up for weakness in the area of feeling.

In any case, the IST– character that was so functional during the previous phase has to be relegated to those component units whose special job it is to be systematic and provide systems for others. The larger organization has to develop the ENF– aspects of its character to prosper at this phase of its growth.

Phase Five: Becoming an Institution

Phase four can last a long time, and in notably successful organizations, it does. It corresponds to the productive middle years of an individual's life. But just as even the most vital person continues to age and eventually slows down, organizations have a natural tendency to turn in a new direction. The vitality of making it slowly gives way to the gravity of becoming an institution.

In this new phase, the organization may continue to be very successful. In a public sense, it may even reach new heights of success. Within its particular industry or profession, it becomes not just a successful organization, but a familiar constellation in the organizational sky. It becomes part of the establishment, and, imperceptibly, it becomes an institution.

To do that, some of its earlier energy is turned back inward (introversion). Patterns of organizationally acceptable practice are established, and radical new ideas are distrusted (sensing–thinking) because everyone agrees that the status quo is pretty darned good. How things are done begins to be more important than what is done. It becomes important to be "one of us," and there is a diminishing concern for productivity or effectiveness. The maverick star may have a great sales record, but the star is not one of us and is eased out the door. The inflexibility of late middle age (sensing–judging) begins to replace the productiveness of early middle age.

The character of this developmental phase is somewhat like that in phase three, but its effect is different because the developmental task here is not to systematize a chaotic venture so that it can continue to grow. Rather, it is to exclude the unpredictable and to insure conformity. Its characteristic form is ISTJ.

Phase Six: Closing In

Phase six is really only a deepening of phase five. The organization not only protects the status quo, it also begins to imitate itself and turns self-imitation into a virtue. Discordant information from the outside—like increasing numbers of complaints or the news that a competitor is launching a new product line—get filtered out or watered down so that it is of little concern. The introversion gets so strong that finally customers are made to feel that the organization is doing them a favor by serving them.

This extreme aversion to customer service takes many forms. If there is a product, a kind of perverse pride in poor quality or poor service may develop—as though service and quality were pandering to weaknesses. If it is a government agency—and many government agencies are firmly ensconced in phase six—the citizen is made to feel that the agency is going out of its way if it even notes a request or a complaint. Paperwork becomes an end in itself, and baroque procedures turn every undertaking into an endurance test for someone who is seeking assistance or information.

Phase Seven: Death

The government agency may be kept alive on the support systems of tax-fed income, but for most other organizations, phase six does not last very long. The organization dies. Its place is taken by a dozen new extraverted ventures, based on an intuitive dream of doing new things and doing them better. And organizational life continues in the same way that individual life continues: One generation disappears and another takes its place.

Character, Change, and Organizational Type

The point at which an organization passes from one growth phase to the next can be a troublesome time. What the great economic historian, R.H. Tawney, wrote about societies is also true of organizations: "The certainties of one age are the problems of the next." The very qualities that got the organization this far become counterproductive.

The passage point between one age and another is a time of far-reaching changes within the organization. The procedures, structures, strategies, and rules of the game must change. The passage point may be catalyzed by external events or it may emerge more organically from the organization's own processes, but in either case it has an intrinsic quality— it's part of the cycle of growth, just as adolescence or midlife are for individuals.

Not all changes are developmental, however. Some simply occur as reactions to the impacts of external forces: A new product or competitor enters the market, new regulations are announced in Washington, another company launches a takeover, or new technology becomes available. These extrinsic changes are not natural to the organizational journey, but, like the intrinsic changes, they challenge the status quo and may force the organization to reorganize, acquire a competitor, lay people off, cut or increase its budget, or seek a new leader.

As I commented in the preface, I first began to experiment with the *Organizational Character Index* in order to assess how organizations were likely to approach and deal with both intrinsic and extrinsic changes. Some of that original interest will have been evident in the descriptions I've given in chapter 3, for those descriptions often refer to how that type of organization approaches or reacts to change. But because this subject is so important in our day of constant organizational turmoil, I want to say some more about character and change in a systematic way.

Change: Extraversion Versus Introversion

Where an organization falls on the spectrum between extreme extraversion and extreme introversion helps to predict some things. All organizations are exposed to extrinsic changes, but extraversion makes an organization more comfortable with that fact. Extraverted organizations carry on a natural dialogue with their environment, picking up cues, testing out responses, and seeking external evaluations of what they are doing. They tend, therefore, to be readier to change in response to external forces.

Introverted organizations are slower to respond to such forces. In fact, they sometimes actively resist responding—and they can turn such slowness into a virtue by describing it as a refusal to "turn with every little breeze." Being more attuned to their own inner processes, they let in external signals more reluctantly and process information from outside more slowly. Since they prefer to work out their responses completely before sharing them, they often show little sign that they have even registered the fact of an external change. When they do register the fact, it is likely to be with some impatience, not just because (like any organization) their plans have been disrupted, but because the external world is always experienced by the introverted organization as to some extent intrusive and as a distraction from the real business that the organization is engaged in.

When a change has taken place, the extraverted organization reorients itself and refashions its ties to the outer world fairly quickly. It may, at least after the fact, treat the change as a stimulant or a corrective: "Best thing that ever happened to us!" The introverted organization is much less likely to view it that way and will probably take much longer to reorient itself and rebuild its external connections after it has been exposed to an outside change.

Intrinsic changes, however, may be easier for the introverted organization to assimilate. Extraverted organizations can be almost immobilized by a developmental passage point like the change from the venture stage to getting organized. They are more likely to be puzzled by internal signs of difficulty, like morale problems or increased levels of turnover. They don't see them coming, they don't process them very well, and they don't recover from them quickly.

Change: Sensing Versus Intuition

Sensing organizations focus on the present and on actuality. That focus acts like a light that illuminates clearly the path that they are on—but only a step ahead. They are like walkers able to move sure footedly and unlikely to twist an ankle, but who have no idea whether the edge of a cliff is a mile away or just a few steps ahead. If the organization is moving quickly, changes in the path may not be foreseen and can bring disaster to the sensing organization.

Intuition, on the other hand, acts like a spotlight with a horizontal beam that scans the territory ahead—but that doesn't cast much light at one's feet. The changes that lie ahead are much more likely to be foreseen, but the intuitive organization is more likely to be tripped up by problems that are right there at their feet. They rightly predict the new technology, but never quite get the details of the current one right.

The same polarity between the organization's sensing and intuitive tendencies is evident in how the two types of organizations go about making a change when they have the choice. Sensing organizations believe in step-by-step change. They talk about the wisdom of incremental change—about how it allows you to keep what is good and improve the rest, how it allows you to make little midcourse corrections without threatening the whole operation, how it holds most variables constant while experimenting with a few. To sensing organizations, incremental change is the only sensible way to change if you have the choice.

Not so for the intuitive organization. There you will hear how piecemeal changes lead to uneven results, how you need an overall design to integrate the whole project, and how you cannot jump a ten-foot ditch one step at a time. The intuitive organization has more faith in the big all-at-once change in which the whole system is transformed.

With their focus on what is actually *there* in a situation, the sensing organization mistrusts such big transformative changes. But that doesn't mean it isn't interested in changing things. It is good at fixing, remodeling, or enhancing how things are already being done. The sensing organization can always make something, including itself, better.

The intuitive organization mistrusts such tinkering and will tell you that a rapidly changing marketplace cannot be dealt with in such a timid fashion. Nothing less than a new vision of things or a whole new model (or, to use a favorite intuitive term, *paradigm*) is sufficient for the scope of change that today demands. With their focus on the possibilities that are under the surface of many situations, intuitive organizations are often aware of new forces, new ideas, and new factors that sensing organizations will not recognize for months.

The flip side of all this is that the intuitive organization is vulnerable to infatuation with its own imaginings. What could be and what will be are not always sufficiently distinct to such an organization. So, for every situation where a highly developed intuitive function made a creative breakthrough possible in technology, operations, or strategy, there are many other situations where the intuitive organization is chasing possibilities that will never be realized. When many possibilities are pursued simultaneously and when they are being constantly tested for workability, the intuitive organization's success rate can be high enough to make it very successful. But when everything is staked on a Great Dream, it is a craps shoot in which the odds do not favor the gambler.

Change: Thinking Versus Feeling

The thinking organization has the natural advantage of finding logical analysis and sequential planning to be almost automatic ways of approaching any new situation. Such an organization also has the advantage of naturally testing outcomes objectively and of being less easily swayed by its own assumptions and wishes. Because it accepts criticism as a necessary step in finding the truth, it tends to subject all plans to a scrutiny that uncovers flaws in data or logic. And because it accepts impersonal measures of outcome, like output and income, it is unlikely to pursue unprofitable courses of action beyond the point where the handwriting appears on the wall.

The feeling organization is loathe to evaluate new situations and the plans to deal with them in such cut-and-dried ways, for the feeling organization insists that the unquantifiable human element is a necessary ingredient in any satisfactory outcome. ("The project didn't make much money, but it sure improved morale!" or "Yes, the service program cost a lot, but look at how we strengthened customer loyalty!")

But there is a reverse side to these matters, as there always is with character and typology. If the feeling organization is not likely to plan things so logically, it usually manages to avoid a common thinking-organization pitfall: forgetting that it is people who have to make any change work. The feeling organization is likely to be more sympathetic to people's reactions to change and to have considered the human side of a change before it is undertaken.

Feeling organizations are more likely to be engaged in change efforts where the impetus has something to do with organizational values. The values are likely to be our values, and they may even be the personal values of the founder. The thinking organization, on the other hand, is likely to be changing because of principles that are simply logical. This difference gives a different tone to the rationale that the two kinds of organizations give for the changes they make: the thinking organization making the logical case and the feeling organization making the sensitive case. Both organizations talk about the right thing to do, but the former means by that the rational or effective thing, while the latter means the humane or wise thing.

The thinking–feeling difference is very important when it comes to the issue of transition. *Transition* is not synonymous with change. (See below for the difference.) Thinking organizations tend to overlook that process, believing that if a change is logical, everyone will accept it and adjust to it—adjustment is itself a thinking concept. Feeling organizations, on the other hand, are likelier to be concerned with the impact of their changes on people and are much quicker to respond to the distress and disruptions that changes cause in any human system.

Change: Judging Versus Perceiving

Judging organizations look at change as a disruptive interlude in what is otherwise the natural organizational state of stability and solidity. "Things were going just fine, but then everything began to change, and...." Perceiving organizations are more likely to see change as the norm and to view times of stasis as islands in the stream. An extremely perceiving character views stability as boring, admonishing that "we need to stir things up a little around here." Thus, perceiving organizations are somewhat fluid, responding to changing situations and tending to mistrust the *unchanging* situation as contrived and inherently unstable. Judging organizations, on the other hand, are uncomfortable with change and hold their breath until they are on solid ground again.

Organizational Type and Transition

Transition is not synonymous with change, but is the psychological process that people go through when they are coming to terms with change.[4] If you move from one city on the East Coast to another on the West Coast, the *change* is the physical relocation, and planning for it involves arranging for transportation, getting your possessions moved, finding a new place to live, and so on. If you have the time, it may take a while, but it can also be accomplished in a matter of days if you do not.

The transition, however, will probably take months, no matter how much of a hurry you are in. It begins before any outward change has occurred, back when you decide to move or learn that you have to move. And it continues long after you arrive at your new home, for the psychological process includes the whole getting-to-know-you process that ends up in making you (finally!) feel at home again.

Whatever the content of the originating change—a new leader or a new computer system, for example—and regardless of whether it is extrinsic or intrinsic, the transition that grows out of it has three overlapping phases. In the first phase , the individual must let go of how things used to be and let go of his or her old identity. This first phase involves ending or losing something. In the second phase, the individual must go through the so-called *neutral zone*, a no-man's-land between the old way of doing things, the old outlook, the old identity, and the new one. This neutral zone is a state that feels chaotic or empty or like a wilderness, but it is also a time when creative solutions to new problems and the discoveries of new answers to old problems are most accessible to people. And, in the third phase, the individual must come out of the neutral zone, taking on a new identity and doing things a new way. In this final phase, people accept what has happened and launch a new beginning based on what they have become.

During the changes in their individual lives, people make their way through these three phases of transition as quickly as they are able to. Sometimes, when what they have to let go of is very close to the core of their being, the transition takes a long time. In such cases, the prospect of letting go may even prove to be too much, and the individual slips into an imaginary world in which the change has simply not taken place.

In an organizational setting, however, the individual has less choice. Orders come down. A deadline is set. The new organizational chart is posted. The computers arrive. The surplus employees are no longer there. To pretend that a change hasn't taken place can cost you your job. But that doesn't keep whole organizations from living for a surprisingly long time in an imaginary world—think of the American auto makers between 1975 and 1985.

Under most circumstances, however, organizations move more quickly than people do. They have to do so in a competitive environment. Because of that, leaders often imagine that because the computers have arrived or because the organizational chart is up on the wall, the people have made the transition or that they will make the transition soon. Or that they will make it if the reasons for the change are explained again—or if they are explained a third time in a loud, threatening voice. But the truth is that until people have gone through the three phases of transition, the change is up for grabs. If they get through the three phases, then they are *there* with a new identity, a new sense of purpose, and a new source of energy to make the new situation work. But today's organizational world is full of changes that looked great and very necessary on paper, but where the people simply haven't let go of the old way—or are lost in the neutral zone. In such cases, people cannot make the new beginning that is essential if the change is really to *take*. Without successful transition, a change is like a transplant that is rejected.

There is no organizational character per se that is either good or bad at managing transition. But each kind of character has its typical pitfalls as well as its typical strengths. And it is to a survey of these that we now turn.

The First Phase of Transition
Losses and Endings: Extraversion Versus Introversion

Every organization and everyone in it has trouble with losses and endings. But extraverted and introverted organizations tend to struggle with different kinds of endings and losses. The extraverted organization, with its outward orientation, is likely to have built its identity around external relations and a public image. If they disappear, it has lost something very vital to its well-being. The introverted organization will also be wounded by such external losses, but it still has a core identity intact and is likelier to rebuild its world. Such an organization is more vulnerable to the loss of a self-image, however.

For example, imagine that two manufacturing organizations, one extraverted and one introverted, each lose a big contract and decide to reorient their strategies away from cutting-edge technology to lower-priced products for the general market. It's the loss of that big customer that will torture the extraverted organization, while the strategic reorientation is just a necessary response. The introverted organization, too, is hurt by the loss of the customer, but what is likely to be really mourned is the loss of its identity as a cutting-edge company.

Losses and Endings: Sensing Versus Intuition

The sensing organization's orientation to the present and to the actual renders it most vulnerable to the loss of the way things are or how they do things. The loss may involve familiar technical procedures, comfortable organizational structures, or other aspects of the status quo. The intuitive organization, being more oriented to the future and to the possible, is more vulnerable to the loss of what they could have done or what they were going to become. It is more vulnerable to the loss of possibilities than to the loss of actualities.

This difference is a subtle one of emphasis, for any organization has difficulty breaking away from both the status quo and something that it was planning to do. All the same, when you can feel people mourning the loss of a dream or a hope for the future, you can assume that the intuitive aspect of the organization has been affected. And when you can feel people mourning the loss of their everyday world, you can assume that the sensing aspect of the organization has been affected.

Losses and Endings: Thinking Versus Feeling

The loss of people affects anyone, and an organization that has had to lay people off, fire a leader, or break up a group that had worked together is going to feel the loss. But thinking organizations accept such losses as part of business. In fact, they often justify them with little homilies about the necessity of being businesslike, cutting costs, working smarter, and so forth. Feeling organizations have more trouble with such justifications and instead react as though they had lost part of their very identity.

Thinking organizations have their own particular vulnerability, however, and that is to the loss of their understanding of what they are doing or the world in which they are doing it. Such organizations try hard to make the world behave logically—that is, according to their explanations of how it is supposed to behave—and are full of distress and disruption when it does not. The financial institution that knows all about economic forces loses something more than profits when interest rates take an unexpected drop; it loses a piece of its intelligible world. A feeling-oriented service organization will also lose something if its investment income drops, but the loss will be different. Its basic identity was never so dependent on its ability to navigate the turbulent currents of rising and falling interest rates, and its "world" of customers is still intact.

Losses and Endings: Judging Versus Perceiving

On one level, you could say that judging organizations are more vulnerable to loss than perceiving organizations because they are more likely to seek out and hold on to stable situations. Being more fluid, perceiving organizations may have less to hold on to and, so, less to lose. After a major reorganization at a very decidedly judging regional telephone company, people complained that they all had new bosses that they had to get used to. At the strongly perceiving Apple Computer, the running joke used to be, "If my manager calls, get his name, will you?"

But on another level, many perceiving organizations are just as identified with the way that they do things as judging organizations are. You can see this fact when a perceiving start-up company running things with a seat-of-the-pants style grows to the point where it needs to establish policies and standard procedures. The family spirit has to give way to roles and hierarchy. Such an organization can go into mourning, and you hear things in the corridors like, "It's no fun around here any more," "We're getting big and impersonal," and "All the creativity and freedom are gone." Perceiving organizations are vulnerable to endings too, but in their own way.

The Second Phase of Transition
The Neutral Zone: Extraversion Versus Introversion

This strange in-between time when things aren't the old way any more but aren't a distinct new way yet either is difficult for everyone and for every organization. It is a time when people feel as though they have been unplugged from their familiar signal systems and left alone in an isolation room. This is especially difficult for extraverted organizations, who may develop problems in their hurry to reestablish their external ties, rushing through the neutral zone so fast that it can't do its work. After all the struggles, such organizations are likely to emerge with cosmetic changes but nothing fundamentally new.

Introverted organizations have their difficulties too, but they are different difficulties. More comfortable with the inward focus that the neutral zone forces upon them, the introverted organization is likelier to look hard at itself and engage in creative self-redefinition. The drawback of the introverted tendency is that its natural inward focus may blind it to changing external realities and make it slow to grasp new external opportunities.

The Neutral Zone: Sensing Versus Intuition

All organizations are vulnerable whenever their ongoing operations and systems are threatened, but sensing organizations find that state a particularly disorienting one. Being dependent on a firm grasp of the actualities of their situation, they are likely to flounder when the actuality is as chaotic and ambiguous as it is in the neutral zone. For them, the limbo state of the neutral zone is more distressing than it is for intuitive organizations.

Intuitive organizations are less vulnerable, for their focus on the future and the possibilities lying under the surface of any ambiguous present gives them something to hold on to. Further, they are less limited than sensing organizations by conventional wisdom about the way things should be. They are, therefore, more likely to be able to capitalize on the neutral zone chaos to come up with a creative solution to their problems.

The drawback to this strength is that they can become so detached from actualities that they confuse their ideas with realities and fail to distinguish their dreams from plans. In the intuitive organization, there is a sense that if something can be imagined, it can be done. That opens many doors that are closed to the sensing organization, but it can also lead to confusion in the neutral zone, where the constraints of the actual are partially removed and anything can be imagined.

If the sensing organization runs the danger of hurrying through the neutral zone because it is so uncomfortable, the intuitive organization runs the danger of forgetting that the neutral zone is only a way station on the path toward a new way of doing things and that possibilities need to be translated into actuality before the organization can benefit from them.

The Neutral Zone: Thinking Versus Feeling

The neutral zone doesn't make very much sense to logical people who see change as a simple matter of heading in a new direction. The notion that the human being needs time (or a time out) in the no-man's-land between the old and the new is not one that corresponds to the categories that most thinking organizations use. Those categories emphasize getting from here to there by the shortest route. (Time is, after all, money.) But organic processes don't run by the clock. Transition is an organic process, not to be hurried any more than cutting teeth or the ripening of grain.

Feeling organizations tend to be a bit more accepting of the neutral zone and the slow reorientation process that is going on there. They are less enamored of the planning chart with its relentless sequence of deadlines. They are less in the thrall of the bottom line, with its coldly arithmetic evaluations of good and bad. And they are more likely to believe that the longer journey that brings the group through intact is finally the shortest line that an organization can take.

The danger that both types of organizations run in the neutral zone is that of growing so distressed that they seek escape at any cost. The thinking organization is more likely to be seduced by an idea that answers the practical need of the moment, but that in the long run leads the organization astray. The feeling organization is more likely to be seduced by a person who seems to know where he or she is going. In either case, seizing the "answer" can get the organization out of the neutral zone—but at the cost of aborting the transition.

The Neutral Zone: Judging Versus Perceiving

With its need for clarity, definition, and closure, the judging organization finds the neutral zone to be a time of miserable confusion. It responds to the chaos with efforts at definition and containment, and to the emptiness with attempts to add new structure and content.

The perceiving organization, on the other hand, will find the neutral zone interesting. In the neutral zone no options are foreclosed. It is a time when it is natural, and even advantageous, to see things in new ways. It is a time to discard the old answers and open things up by brainstorming twenty new answers. The emptiness that distressed the judging organization looks very much like freedom to the perceiving, and the chaos that was repugnant to the judging penchant for clear definition looks to the perceiving organization like pure energy.

The Last Phase of Transition:
The New Beginning: Extraversion Versus Introversion

To the extraverted organization, a new beginning means getting back into a vital and productive relationship with the external world of customers, suppliers, competitors, and regulators. When that is done, the extraverted organization feels that it's finally back on track. The introverted organization sees a new beginning differently, viewing it as a time of renewed energy and purpose and a renewed sense of organizational identity. As far as they go, both types of organizations are "right" in what they believe and "wrong" to think that the other half of the truth is unimportant or that it will take care of itself. The extraverted organization needs to pay more attention to its identity, and the introverted organization needs to pay more attention to its environment.

Coming out of a period in the neutral zone, the extraverted organization may feel the need to conduct some external activity—a market survey or a series of visits with key customers. The introverted organization will probably be more attracted to the idea of an organizational retreat where a project is planned to get people aligned with the organization's new purpose.

The New Beginning: Sensing Versus Intuition

The intuitive organization is likely to turn to visioning exercises when it seeks to launch a new beginning. A mental image of how-we-will-be is the core around which intuitive efforts are built, and without such an image the efforts have little cohesion. The sensing organization, on the other hand, will probably view such visioning as all very well (if you have the time) but believe that the real question involves what we'll all do on Monday to get this thing rolling. The sensing organization is energized by action and by getting started. The intuitive organization is energized by imagining and by planning how to get started.

The details of reporting relationships and of the operational procedures are make-or-break issues for the sensing organization, while the intuitive organization believes that those things can be worked out later and that what needs attention now is the overall design and the big picture. Until that is settled, there is no larger context within which the details mean anything. Sensing organizations want a clear destination too, although they believe that that is pretty easy to settle on—and once you get going on a path you find that you keep making those incremental course changes, and that before you know it you are heading in some new direction anyway.

The New Beginning: Thinking Versus Feeling

Thinking is impersonal, feeling personal. So it is natural that the thinking organization gravitates toward explaining roles and principles, while the feeling organization defines relationships and values. The latter seeks to give people a place and a group to belong to, while the former believes that people basically need a task to do and an understanding of the collective mission. The thinking organization treats the new beginning as an exercise in launching new systems, while the feeling organization views it as an exercise in activating new collaborative efforts.

The New Beginning: Judging Versus Perceiving

The judging organization is relieved to launch a new beginning—almost regardless of what it involves. To be out of the quicksand of the neutral zone and onto the solid ground of a new chapter in the organization's life is a relief to any organization that likes things clear, firm, and definite. The perceiving organization has mixed feelings. Not that it likes confusion and inefficiency, but the very qualities that make the new beginning a relief to the judging organization feel too much to the perceiving organization like the first signs that a rut is being formed. The new policy, the new work teams, the new office layout: All of these things convey a sense of routine, and the perceiving organization doesn't like it much. Before long, you'll hear talk about "the good old days" when everything was up for grabs, when no one had a clear job description, and when they were all in the mess together.

Conclusion

Character shapes not only how the organization sees change but also how (and even whether) it deals with transition. As with all matters involving typology, there aren't good characters and bad characters. There are simply the strengths and weaknesses of the particular character that an organization has. Neither extraversion nor introversion, thinking nor feeling, sensing nor intuition, judging nor perceiving is better than the other—except in particular circumstances.

The only generalization that you can make is that the best capacity of all is to be able to honor both ends of these polarities—each in its appropriate time. But few organizations have developed the capacity to do that. Instead, they are captive to their characters. The question of how to escape that captivity is the topic of the next chapter.

Chapter Five

Character and Organizational Development

Much that passes for organizational development is really little more than organizational repair. In fact there are really only two kinds of activity that deserve to be called organizational development. The first is the activity of unfolding the inherent potentialities of the organization's basic character and compensating for its weaknesses so that those potentialities can be realized. The second is the activity of helping the organization to move through the natural phases of growth so that it can bear the fruit of its maturity. Real organizational development is not simply team building, conflict resolution, fostering creativity and visioning, or any of the other activities normally considered in the cadre of organizational development. It involves those activities only if they are carried out in the context of one of the two aforementioned larger, genuinely developmental efforts.

The development of, let's say, an ESTJ organization is a different task from the development of an INFP organization. Not only do they have potentialities characterized by quite opposite strengths and weaknesses, they also have very different problems as they move through the developmental course of the organizational life cycle.

The failure to appreciate these differences—which begins with the lack of any reliable way to understand and assess them—accounts for a common but often baffling failure: The communications project that worked so well at First National Bank bombs at Second National; the alignment exercise that got Alpha Software back on track falls flat at Omega Software; and the MBTI work with the executive team that reduced the conflict at City Hospital had little effect on the comparable group at County Hospital.

Assessing an organization's character is the essential first step in any developmental effort. The second step is helping the leadership of the organization to understand the developmental implications of that type of character. Designing a development plan for the organization, in collaboration with the leadership, is the third step in the effort. The final step is undertaking some of those interventions that people usually refer to as OD work. Since we've already discussed the assessment piece in chapters 2 and 3, let's move on to the task of understanding the developmental implications of whatever you have found.

Organizational Self-acceptance Is Important

Anyone who has taken the *Myers-Briggs Type Indicator* is likely to remember the peculiar mixture of excitement and chagrin at seeing his or her own tendencies right there in black and white. The chagrin comes from having one's foibles and vulnerabilities so clearly described. The chagrin is tempered, however, by the recognition that these "defects" are not simply personal and blameworthy. They are weaknesses that are a natural aspect of your type, not of you personally. They are like the grain of a particular wood, the very value of which carries with it some related drawback: Balsa is light but not very strong, oak is strong but heavy—and so on. Many weaknesses are nothing more than the flip side of strengths.

The excitement that people usually experience when they read their MBTI type description is twofold. First, it is exciting to see weaknesses in this light and to realize that they are neither reprehensible nor fatal flaws. They can be steered around and compensated for. Second, it is exciting to see so clearly what one's natural strengths are. There are no bad types. Every type has its intrinsic strengths and can look forward to success and fulfillment if its typological strengths are developed and capitalized on and if its weaknesses are strengthened or counteracted.

People who are closely identified with an organization usually feel the same mixture of chagrin and excitement when they read the description of its character. As with individual typology, self-understanding leads to self-acceptance. And self-acceptance leads to paths through which the natural limitations of character can be transcended. Like individuals, organizations can become better only by first accepting how they characteristically are.

This path toward organizational improvement runs counter to the generic prescriptions that are being made today by all the business best-sellers. Whether it is the eight features of excellence or the four attributes of good leadership, such prescriptions are offered as though they were equally relevant and applicable to all organizations. What I am arguing is that a particular organization needs its own recipe for success, one that is consonant with its inherent character. As with individuals, organizations need to become fully *themselves*, not somebody or something else.

A case in point: the Gillette Co. During the eighties it was under constant attack, fighting off four takeover attempts—one of them by the narrowest of margins. Now, just a few years later, Gillette is very profitable again, and it has become so (in the words of a *Forbes Magazine* writer) "by reasserting the principles that had made this old multinational company great in the first place and which were in danger of being lost."[1]

Gillette's original Safety Razor had been a technological breakthrough, and Gillette had historically drawn upon the introverted power of its technological excellence. But in the 1970s the industry changed. Bic, an extraverted marketing champ, introduced disposable razors, and Gillette followed Bic's lead and tried to compete on alien ground. It got lost in the crowd, so it did an about-face, pulled its money out of advertising disposables, and put it into developing the Sensor razor and reestablishing its identity as a maker of first-class shaver systems.

Organizational Self-denial Is Dangerous

Individuals who deny some aspect of their own makeup have a tendency to project that quality onto someone else. The rigidly self-righteous moralist, who denies all his or her own baser impulses, sees them in others. The tough guy, whose own feelings are buried under layers of denial, complains that everyone else is "soft." Perennial adolescents, playing their way through life, claim that others are uptight. In Jungian terms, this denied-and-projected aspect of the individual is the person's *shadow*. The shadow is a natural phenomenon that is created not by dishonesty but by the fact that the light of awareness can only illumine the side of the person that it shines on. The other side, like the dark side of the moon, is in the shadow. Individuals can become aware of this dark side, can study it, can learn from it, and can round themselves out in the process. But many individuals do not do this, preferring instead to deny their shadow and to see it only by projecting it onto someone else.

Organizations do the same thing. The no-nonsense, by-the-numbers operations division of a large corporation sees its own denied and undeveloped concern for people as "the problem with the Human Resources Department." They describe HR as touchy-feely and full of bleeding hearts, and who think the production objectives operations has set for itself are less important than "hand-holding" the people. (Needless to say, the HR department does its own reverse projections, in which *its* denied and undeveloped objectivity and concern for results are discovered in the "harsh," "impersonal" "widget makers" over in operations.) That kind of projection goes on throughout large corporations, as one division or department discovers its shadow in some other entity that it has to work with: R&D and manufacturing, the home office and the field organization, finance and marketing.

You might pause here and think about your own functional specialty and how its representatives, including you, view people in very different specialties. The surest sign that you have stumbled over your shadow is that you find you are always frustrated by or antagonistic toward some other area of the organization.

The same thing goes on between the whole company or institution and its competition. The latter may be transformed (through projection) from tough competitors into cruel exploiters or unscrupulous manipulators. The innovative company that is a little weak in the area of sales and customer relations is likely to see its competitor as "just a bunch of salespeople" willing to promise anything but who "don't even understand their own technology." And the church, whose services are built around thoughtful sermons, may view the elaborate ritual in the church across town as an indication that "the people over there just repeat meaningless phrases" and that they "just believe what they are told."[2]

Shadow projecting is as natural with organizations as it is with individuals and, if people in the organization are aware of what projection can do and are careful to remember to compensate for it, is not dangerous. Unfortunately, such care and awareness are not common. Organizations instead really believe that what they project is actually out there. The result is that most organizations exist in an environment that is greatly distorted by self-projected shadow images.[3]

Needless to say, such perceptual distortions lead to dangerous conclusions. With competitors, they lead to misassessments of actual strengths and weaknesses as well as failures to be ready for circumstances that are actually somewhat predictable. With departments or divisions that are part of the same larger corporation or institution, these perceptual distortions lead to serious communication problems and power struggles that make everyday dealings difficult and render effective collaboration impossible.

Reclaiming the Organizational Shadow

The first task of real organizational development is to deal with the organizational shadow. This involves both education and training. The education is to alert leaders and managers to the problem of the organizational shadow and the dangers of projection. The training is to strengthen the organization's undeveloped characteristics—the dark side of its moon.

Without such developmental training, organizations faced with difficulty fall back on their tried and true answers and work themselves deeper into their difficulties. Polaroid has done this, and so has Control Data. Both were introverted powerhouses that had grown successful through their technological resources. But then their markets changed. The tide ran toward marketers like Kodak and IBM. As *Boardroom Reports* recently noted, both Polaroid and Control Data lost ground "because their preoccupation with research and development [an INT– activity] is yielding products nobody wants. They're not relying enough on marketing to find out what consumers really want."[4] They need to develop their shadow side, which is ESF–.

If you are working with the operations group (thinking), the strengthening of the shadow side may involve training in human relations (feeling). If you are working with the intuitive–feeling human resources group, however, it may involve some training in effective sensing–thinking business practices. With the sensing–thinking finance people, it may be something on appreciating the qualitative measurements of success (which are intuitive–feeling), and for the home office it may be something on letting go of control (they are so thinking–judging!) so that others can exercise it.

It is often effective, when two groups are projectively polarized, to set up a training exercise where they switch identities so that each can experience what it is like to be the other one. This can be done by having each group do the following:

- List adjectives and nouns that they would use to describe themselves
- List adjectives and nouns that they would use to describe the other group
- List adjectives and nouns that they imagine the other group might use to describe them

The lists are then exchanged, and each group reflects on how the situation looks from the other side. Finally, both groups are given descriptions (from chapter 3) of their own character and that of the shadow group. These are discussed, first within each group, and then together.

Groups that take part in this exercise are usually startled by the correspondence between their lists and the descriptions of the organizations' different characters. The exercise helps a group in two ways: First, it helps to depolarize the groups, and, second, it suggests an agenda for the future development of each group.

Conflict resolution techniques, like active listening, are useful when two characterologically different groups are locked in a shadow dance of the sort we are describing. Active listening involves a dialogue on a problematic topic between representatives of each group, in which each side must repeat accurately what representatives of the other group have said before answering it. Sometimes these procedures are supplemented with the requirement that each group representative withhold a reply until she or he has put into words the unspoken concerns and attitudes that might lie behind the words of the other side.

With all such techniques, it is important to go beyond getting antagonistic groups to listen to one another and to help them to understand how their misunderstandings happen. If you are working with a single organizational client, this is easier to do by beginning with how another organization misunderstands your client and then extending that insight to the question of how your client projects its own shadow onto the other, too.

Character and Mergers/Acquisitions

These matters are particularly important whenever two different organizations are being combined through merger, acquisition, or (if they are components of the same corporation or institution) reorganization. Such combinations juxtapose different character types in much the same way that a marriage juxtaposes two different personal typologies. For that reason, consultation in that kind of situation becomes a kind of organizational "couples counseling" in which each party is helped to understand a whole cluster of things:

- How and why the other is different—and that the difference is legitimate
- How the world, including one's own organization, looks through the other's eyes
- How one's perception of the world, the other, and oneself is shaped by one's own character-based outlook
- How each organization actually needs the other—even in cases where one is the dominant partner and the other is not so powerful—because each represents the other's undeveloped side
- How the combination can be effected in such a way that the strengths of both are protected and serve to compensate for the others' weaknesses

Rules of Thumb for the Development of an Organization's Undeveloped Side

As you saw in chapter 3, the combination of the four basic aspects of an organization into sixteen groupings gives considerable subtlety to the concept of *character*. And that, in turn, makes the characterological approach to organizational development too complicated to summarize in a few pages. Nonetheless, some generalizations may be useful.

Guidelines For Extraverted and Introverted Organizations

Extraverted organizations generally need to develop their capacity to use their own inner signals for guidance rather than taking their cues exclusively from external sources. They also need to be more tolerant of neutral zone situations where a time of inwardness is needed before deciding how to respond to external stimuli with action or communication. This may require that change projects be slowed down a little.

Introverted organizations usually need to take the external world of customers and competitors more seriously. They need to remember to bring other people into the decision-making process rather than waiting until a decision is reached and then trying to sell it to them. Such organizations also need to work hard to maintain contact with their several external and internal constituencies and to keep them informed, especially when things are moving forward slowly.

Example: I met recently with an organizational development specialist from a very successful, young, high-tech company. She had worked earlier for an older, bigger and also very successful high-tech company, and she was puzzled over the difference between the two companies. Her former employer was a decidedly introverted company that had wonderfully creative talent and a heritage of great products. But these products always had to be sold to a market that did not understand them or how much they could benefit from them. That company had never done very sophisticated marketing because it hadn't needed to. But recently, increasing competition had changed that. As she said, "all we worked on during my last year there was trying to get people to take the customer seriously." In our terms, they had been trying to develop more extraversion. Her present employer, the newer company, was a different case: It was founded by a marketing executive who wasn't even sure initially what business he wanted to be in. He studied the marketplace and then chose what he took to be a promising niche. "My present employers," the woman said, "are whizzes at marketing, but I can't get them to pay attention to what is going on inside the company." In the terms we are using, the younger company was extraverted and needed to develop its introverted side. Starting with that, we put together a plan for helping the new company develop its shadow side that was the opposite of what her former employer had needed.

Guidelines for Sensing and Intuitive Organizations

Sensing organizations need to develop their capacities to pick up clues about what the future is likely to bring, as well as about the potentialities that are under the surface of the present. They need to reinforce their ability to see the big picture, the underlying design, the dominant trend behind the details. They also need to remind themselves that their preferred incremental style of change will prove to be inadequate to deal with the big turning points in an organization's life. At such times a change that is more holistic and transformational is needed. To be ready for such times, the sensing organization needs to develop its tolerance for and appreciation of the intuitive, nonlinear, symbolic modes of thought rather than dismissing them because they don't fit with assumptions or aren't supported by hard data. Sensing organizations also need to be a little looser when they are following a set plan lest their tendency toward taking all the right steps may make them unaware of unexpected developments or anomalous events that don't fit with expectations.

Intuitive organizations need to develop the capacity to gather, process, and use information effectively—and to take its implications seriously rather than opting for hunches or flashes of insight to light the way. They also need to be able to discriminate more effectively between an *interesting possibility* and a *good idea*, and to be willing to forego the pursuit of the former if they turn out not to qualify as the latter.[5] To do that, intuitive organizations need to work out details more completely before actions are undertaken. They also need to spell them out more fully in communications and to be less impatient of people who need more information before they are ready to act.

Example: Kodak and Polaroid, recent antagonists in a huge legal action, represent companies that need to move in opposite directions. Kodak held a near monopoly on the photography market for decades, and true to its *sensing* character, spent little time developing radically new technologies. Why should it focus on mere possibilities when what it was already doing was so successful? Polaroid, on the other hand, had built its business out of actualizing such possibilities—first with polarizing sunglasses and then with an instant camera. But in later years, possibilities were not adequately checked against actual consumer interest: Witness the instant movie camera that no one was interested in buying.

Guidelines For Thinking and Feeling Organizations

Thinking organizations need to remember that all of their systems and procedures are dependent on human beings and that human beings do not live by reason alone. They need to develop ways to incorporate feeling into their operations by working to enhance the motivation of individuals and the harmony of groups. To that end, they need to develop the capacity to communicate with the heart as well as the head and to respond to people supportively as well as critically. As they plan strategically, they need to build in a way of assessing the human implications (both inside and outside the organization) of the paths of action they are considering. And they need to build in to their standard decision-making criteria a greater concern for the human costs of organizational outcomes.

Feeling organizations need to develop ways to balance their inherent awareness of the personal dimension of situations with one in which other factors carry significant weight. To this end, they need to clarify their principles so that compassion does not destroy fairness and every individual situation does not send the decision-making process back to Go. They need, further, to develop their capacity to critique ideas logically and to act in spite of the fact that there is a likelihood of some individual distress or group disharmony. Finally, they need to develop policies that insure that relationships do not carry undue weight in the organization.

Example: Two large manufacturing companies exemplify the thinking–feeling polarity in the differences between their definitions of quality. Like many of today's companies, they had both put a heavy emphasis on improving quality. To the thinking company, that meant reducing defects in numbers per hundred thousand and an elaborate mechanistic system for monitoring that ratio. (Whether or not the quantitative perfection pleased customers was never very clear.) To the feeling company, quality meant meeting customer expectations, so they set up an 800 number staffed with sympathetic operators—though whether the products were ever improved by the complaint-borne information was unclear. Not too surprisingly, the feeling company evaluated my own company's training programs by asking participants how they'd rate them, even though such "feel-great" measures don't necessarily tell you whether the program really helped anyone. The thinking company would have been appalled at such soft-headedness: They measured participants *transition management skills* before and after they took the seminar. Unfortunately, the company never managed to get a solid grasp of what skills were needed to manage transition—but they did come out with indisputable figures. Each company, you could argue, did half the job of quality improvement (and training assessment) very well.

Guidelines for Judging and Perceiving Organizations

Judging organizations must be sure to develop effective ways to pick up signals and clues from the external environment—and from the inner environment as well. Further, they need to build in checks on their tendency to interpret and act upon such information too quickly—especially before data is complete enough to reveal the real situation. They need to be careful that clarity of definition in statements and policies is not achieved at the price of excluding ambiguous data or ambivalent impulses. And judging organizations must guard against the tendency to follow schedules blindly, even when they are no longer relevant to external situations or inner desires.[6] Finally, judging organizations need to guard against rigidity in the interpretation of their own rules, watching that compliance with the letter of the law does not destroy the spirit behind the law.

Perceiving organizations need to build in more predictability, definition, and structure so that successes can be more effectively replicated and failures more foreseeably avoided. Planning capacities need to be enhanced, as does the ability to improve routine operations: the first to lay out a clear path to follow, and the second to avoid doing things in careless or impetuous ways. Finally, perceiving organizations need to develop more appreciation for areas of stability and forego some of the joys of fluidity and responsiveness. They need to settle down, just as judging organizations need to lighten up.

Example: Seldom do you get as sharp a contrast between the developmental needs at the opposite ends of this polarity as you do in John Sculley's autobiographical *Odyssey*, where he describes moving from the judging Pepsico to the perceiving Apple. At the former, senior management meetings were held around a 21-foot-long table of burnished Carpathian elm. Everyone, wearing blue pinstripe suits and red ties, sat by rank around the table—with lower-ranked executives seated in an outer ring around the walls. The agenda was prescribed, and the meeting was devoted to formal reports, illustrated with large graphs showing discrepancies between projected and actual sales figures. The meeting ran to a tight schedule. Then there was Apple, where Sculley describes his first executive session thus:

> I tried to direct the discussion around these and other issues placed on the agenda, but it was to no avail. The meeting became a free-for-all. Whoever could attract the group's attention controlled the floor. It was difficult to distinguish between facts and opinions. People would have side conversations during executive presentations; some would get up from their places to get something. It was virtually impossible to keep order.[7]

With each of these issues, the task is not to change an organization into its opposite—something that would be impossible to do anyway. Rather, the task is to develop the undeveloped capacity of the organization so that it can choose between what it does easily and naturally and what it has learned to do with some difficulty. In the final analysis, I suspect, it is not the capacity to be intuitive or sensing, judging or perceiving. It is instead the capacity to maintain a tension between both of these apparently opposite characters that represents organizational health.

The Tactics of Organizational Development

Organizations have more freedom in strengthening and compensating for the weaknesses of their own character than individuals do. We have already noted that the organization's leader or its leadership group is a major determinant of its character, and the leadership can be changed. The change of leadership, at the top of the whole organization or at one of its component units or departments, is a time-honored way of turning the organization in a new direction. But this is seldom done with much awareness of character.

It is assumed that a new leader will make changes and improve things. Such substantive changes may, indeed, take place. But the larger and too often overlooked issue is how the new leader will bend the organization's character in a new direction. Such bending is at least as important as the specific changes: Witness the enormous remodeling that Jack Welch is carrying out at General Electric, a remodeling that is partly a physical reorganization and is also, at a deeper level, a push in the direction of an ENTJ character.

We have noted that the typological makeup of a staff or an employee pool is a major characterological determinant, and that too can be changed. The young start-up company which is trying to develop a more business-like approach to delivering its services can help itself by hiring people who tend toward the ISTJ and away from the ENFP corner of the type table. (My own INTJ consulting business has been immeasurably strengthened by finding new employees with strongly developed extraversion, sensing, and feeling.)

If history cannot be changed, its interpretation can. Leaders can recast the past in a new light, emphasizing some of its elements and playing down others—and, in the process, can influence still another determinant of organizational character. In the process, the founder—yet another element—may be understood quite differently, with significant implications for the organizational character. I think that it is no accident Henry Ford's rather severe limitations as a person and a leader have become much more common knowledge at a time when the company he founded has been trying to break away from the ISTJ character that he established.

Add to all of these possibilities the way in which the weak shadow characteristics can be identified and strengthened through education and training, and one has the basic ingredients of a true organizational development effort.

Life Cycle Development

These ways of influencing the organization's character take on a particularly developmental flavor when they come at one of the passage points in the organization's life cycle discussed in the last chapter. Here is a brief review of the first four of those passage points, together with the kinds of developmental activity that may be helpful at each.

From the Dream to the Venture

The dream is inside the dreamer and is by its nature very fluid. To be realized as a *venture*, there needs to be extraversion to bring it out and judging to give it organizational form. Young organizations rightly use customer visits, business planning, and manufacturing specifications to strengthen whatever extraversion and judging there are in the organization. They often hire people with business experience to do the same thing.

From the Venture to Getting Organized

The venture is likely to be very possibility-oriented. It isn't much yet, but the whole idea is that it *could* become something big and important. That represents the intuitive part of the venture. The developmental task of the venture is to explore the viability of and the market responses to the venture. So extraversion is important. But if and as the venture grows, it gets too complicated for the seat-of-the-pants way of doing things and the willingness to respond to whatever the market presents as an opportunity. Its need to get organized forces it to develop its internal systems (introversion) and to standardize its operations so that policies and procedures can be developed and monitored (sensing). This is the time of work-flow analyses and of financial forecasting. Ventures can't tell you what a project costs or how long it will take, but when the organization moves into getting organized, it must develop the capacity to do these things. The developmental activities that are essential are largely technical: establishing data bases, training in budget procedures, and generating policy statements.

From Getting Organized to Making It

Getting organized provides the controls and information systems to permit the organization to grow. But as the organization begins to do that, people are likely to feel that they have lost something. This is the time you hear them idealizing the old days when things were just starting to get going. Development requires that after things get organized, a new spirit of extraversion returns to the organization to turn its attention back to its market. (This is when customer service programs are helpful.) Intuition is needed to see the possibilities inherent in its situation, and it is useful at this point to clarify the vision and to strengthen the organization's marketing capability.

From Making It to Becoming an Institution

While the organization is engaged in making it, its energy is focused outward toward its markets and toward not just what is actually there but toward what could be created. But as time passes and if the organization continues to grow, it becomes part of the establishment in business or industry. Leaders often like the clout of this new organizational status and the trappings that go with it. To cultivate these things, the focus will slowly turn inward (introversion). How something is done begins to be almost as important as what is done, and common practices begin to be formalized into patterns that not only get the job done but turn it into a minor kind of ritual. (Intuition begins to give way to sensing.) The openness to opportunity and the readiness to seize it begin to give way to a spirit of consolidating gains and shoring up defenses against loss. (If there was any perceiving drive in the organization, it rapidly disappears and a strong judging character replaces it.)

Development, Character, and Renewal

Not all organizations try or even want to become institutions. The phase of *making it* is the dynamic midpoint of the organizational life cycle, and thereafter there is a subtle sense of deceleration even though the organization may still be growing and becoming more powerful. So some organizations seek to arrest their development when they have made it. They continue at that point to enhance the strengths and compensate for the weaknesses of the organization's inherent character.

When an organization has entered the institutional phase of its life cycle, it has reached a developmental crossroads. Thereafter, the path of least resistance is toward phase six, *closing in*—and, after that, toward phase seven, *death*. But there is still another developmental choice for the organization. Because there is no biological aging process going on, organizations are far more able than individuals to turn back the developmental clock. That is, they can, to some degree, return to an earlier life phase. At least they can do so until they become fully ensconced in the closing-in phase.

Turning back the clock is actually a kind of redevelopment, a renewal of the energy and spirit that characterized some earlier phase of the organizational life cycle. Such redevelopment can take different forms.

Generating a New Dream

Renewal can involve the generation of a new dream for some part of or even the whole organization. When you hear people saying they need a new vision, this is what they are calling for. Dreams are most likely to emerge from those parts of the organization that are closest in character to the IN–P of the dream. If such parts do not exist, a team can be formed and sent away to an unstructured time and place in which introversion is encouraged, intuition is stimulated, and judging is discouraged. British Petroleum's Engineering Technology Center in London did this when it reinvented itself as a customer-service function rather than as a research and development group.[8]

Launching New Ventures

Renewal can also come by launching new ventures or by breaking down large institutional entities into separate and self-supporting ventures. To do either of these things is to build and nurture an EN–J character. That is what Jack Welch has been doing at GE, whose traditional character had been set by the historical dominance of ISTJ finance.[9] Campbell Soup tried to do the same thing by dividing its large divisions into small product-based business units. The current wave of reorganizations from functional department–based organizations into strategic-business-unit–based organizations is a move in this direction.

Recovering Lost Energies of an Earlier Phase

Renewal may also simply involve trying to recross the passage point that separates institutionalism from making it and recovering the lost energies of that earlier phase. That is what companies are trying to do when they launch total quality or customer service programs, or when they undertake major marketing or research and development efforts. Donald Peterson's major campaign at Ford to improve quality, use cross-disciplinary teams (e.g., the Taurus design group), and enhance customer service is an example of this kind.

Acquiring External Ventures or Organizations

Sometimes those who want to renew the organization choose not to work with their own resources but to acquire external ventures or organizations in an early stage of the making-it phase in hopes that the new partner will breathe new life into the old. General Motors did this when it bought EDS and tried (or is still trying) to integrate that younger company's electronic expertise and entrepreneurial energies with its own institutional resources.

Because all of these efforts juxtapose the old and the new, they usually have the pitfalls of the May-December marriage, where the aging partner is trying to incorporate the youthful energy of the other. Whatever the practical rationale for and gains from such a union, there is a two-sided problem with it. First, the senior partner is likely to be highly ambivalent about the character of the junior. This shows up in many merger/acquisition situations, and it also shows up internally whenever a corporation seeks to incorporate new entrepreneurial ventures into its regular organizational system. (According to a recent *Wall Street Journal* article, Kodak has just given up on a long effort to do this with several dozen ventures that had originally looked very promising.) Second, the junior partner is likely to begin by feeling hopeful and excited, but to end by feeling exploited when it becomes clear that its real task is to "breathe new life" into an organization that is very ambivalent about revitalization.[10]

The Pitfalls of Organizational Development

Organizations, where the underlying character and the growth phase combine to make introverted intuition a dominant characteristic, have a tendency to turn to *visioning* whenever there is some question of where they are going or what they really are. Organizations where extraverted sensing is the developmentally and intrinsically dominant characteristic will often turn to *benchmarking*, that is, modeling themselves on other companies who do some particular thing very well as a way to determine how things ought to be done.

Each is the natural path of inquiry for that particular character, and it may be a productive one. But one should always question whether it may not be simply the familiar path and whether it may not lead to answers that are either already known or fail to address squarely the real organizational need. Visioning may be the better solution for the extraverted sensing organization, and benchmarking for the introverted intuitive.

Don't forget, however, that this kind of "shadow" strategy always needs to be presented to the organization in terms that its natural character can grasp. So, for example, visioning needs to be presented with examples from other organizations (because extraverted organizations find such external evidence convincing), and benchmarking needs to be presented as a new possibility and a way of drawing out the best inherent resources of the organization (because that is what the introverted organization always seeks to do).

Conclusion

There are, therefore, three important contributions that the concept of organizational character can make to the field and the task of organizational development. The first is the assistance it provides in understanding what kinds of help the organization needs in order to capitalize on and compensate for its inherent character. The second is the insight it provides into what the organization needs at its particular point in the life cycle to move ahead along the path of development or back toward redevelopment. The third is a character-based understanding of the organization's resistance to those developmental efforts that are made under the first and second contributions and the way it helps to define the kinds of communication that will be most successful in counteracting that resistance.

Underlying all three contributions is the recognition that organizations, like individuals, have inherent characteristics that must be understood and respected if real growth is to take place.

Chapter Six

Organizational Character and Individual Type

Using Individual Type Within the Organization

One of the advantages that organizational character, based on psychological type, has over corporate culture is that it can be reliably correlated with the *Myers-Briggs Type Indicator*. Consultants have long used the MBTI in organizations for career counseling, team building, and leadership development.[1]

In career counseling, individual type is compared with the typical patterns of professional or business specialties—accountants, surgeons, counselors, advertising executives, and so on—to see how the person fits with the type that is dominant in that particular field.[2] For example: –ST– types make up more than half of the MBTI samples of accountants and bank employees. –SF–s fill eight out of ten sales and customer relations jobs. –NF–s dominate the field of counseling, and –NT–s populate the nation's research labs.

A typological correspondence with the character of a particular field or profession doesn't guarantee anything, of course, but it is suggestive and useful. It helps, first, in understanding the tension people sometimes experience between their role or task and their inner preferences—a tension that if great enough may lead to a career change. Second, it helps to steer a person within a field to those areas where he or she would feel most comfortable. The INTJ nurse might do best in a research facility or as a teacher. The ENFP banker (if there are such) would probably be more successful in the human resources department or customer service than in records or foreclosures.

In team building, all the members of a particular work team take the MBTI and the results are grouped to show the team's strengths and weaknesses. Many teams are narrow in their typology, both because the task may attract primarily a certain type and because the manager or leader may have the tendency to select his or her own type in choosing new recruits. The team's weaknesses can be offset by adding people of other types, particularly types that do naturally those things that the team is having difficulty doing. The team dominated by introversion is likely to have trouble connecting with other groups and could use some extraverts. The team dominated by thinking will probably keep overlooking the human dimensions of its decisions and could use some feeling types.

The MBTI profile of the team is also useful in identifying and explaining the characteristic conflicts that occur within the team. By relating these conflicts to differences in styles of perceiving and decision making, many conflict areas can be depersonalized. ("She really doesn't have it in for me. She just sees the world differently from the way I do!") And as people come to understand those of different types, they also learn how best to communicate and argue constructively with them. The intuitive learns to give examples and to include accurate data, for example, when debating a point with a sensing colleague.

In leadership development, individual type is used to categorize people's natural styles of leading or managing others. In this way, individuals can be educated as to their strengths and weaknesses in working with subordinates of different types. In one of my client organizations, an INTJ leader very quickly came to see that his naturally logical but cryptic I'm-only-going-to-say-this-once communication style was extremely painful to people in his ISFJ organization. While he did not become a new person, he taught himself to slow down, spell things out more carefully, ask for reactions, and listen.

In each of these areas, the application of MBTI information about individuals to an organizational setting provides immensely valuable and otherwise unavailable insights into why individuals and groups either do or do not work together effectively. And it provides the basis for educational, staffing, and career development efforts to improve personal and interpersonal effectiveness.

Adding the Variable of Organizational Character

Information about organizational character supplements these three efforts, for it enables us to determine with some objectivity the characteristics of the organization that the career is being pursued in, that the team is serving, and that the leader is trying to lead. And it enables us to do so not only in terms of the organization's intrinsic character but also in terms of the characteristic demands that will be made on everyone by virtue of the organization's place in its life cycle.

Readers who want to find out the implications of their own MBTI type for their career, for their relation to some team of which they are a part, or for some leadership role that they play in an organizational setting should consult the books listed in Appendix B. What I shall do is to suggest how people with that kind of information can use data on the character of their organization to develop even greater insight than is gained from the MBTI alone.

Character and Career

Most of the available MBTI-related work on careers deals with the field that a particular type tends to select. As important as that information is, it's utility is limited by the fact that many people work in organizations whose character is different from that of their career field. So the field itself may tell only part of the story of one's suitability for a given line of work in an actual organizational context. A person may be an accountant, for example, but she works for an architectural firm. Or he may be a manager, but he works for a hospital. Or he may be a clerk, but he works for a field station of the US Forest Service. Or she may be a career counselor, but she works for a big manufacturing company. In all of these cases, the organization—which has a very different character from the person's vocational category—will influence his or her effectiveness and satisfaction as much as the type of work being done.

Any single career category may fit quite differently into two different organizations. The same nurse (an ISFP, let's say) may have a strikingly different career experience working at an INTJ college, an ISTJ big-city hospital, an ESTJ factory, or an ISFJ rural clinic. The nurse's career, in other words, is not only a personal/professional path, but also a relationship between a particular individual and a specific organization—more likely these days, a sequence of specific organizations.

Career development is thus dyadic, like the development of a marriage or other significant relationship. The *other* in this relationship is an organization and not an individual. Understanding the character of the organization enables you to go beyond questions of whether an individual is in the right field to the additional question of whether the person is pursuing a given kind of work within the right organization.

Yet saying it that way is misleading, for, as with a marriage, it is not simply a question of whether the two types "fit," but of how the similarities and differences between the individual and the organization shape the relationship. Neither the individual nor the organization would necessarily be well served if people's MBTI types and the character of their organizations were identical. Like a two-peas-in-the-pod marriage, the result would probably be comfortable but not necessarily very interesting or growthful for the person, and definitely not as effective for the organization as a relation in which there were some significant differences between the individual and the organization.

Both individuals and organizations can profit greatly from relating to differences, for it is through such differences that each is balanced out and helped to develop. Any organization's character, whatever it is, automatically guarantees that it has characteristic weak suits and that it has a tendency to back itself into characteristic corners. The organization needs individuals with complementary types to round itself out and to compensate for its own inherent weaknesses. But the need is reciprocal, for it is only in situations in which individuals are pushed to move outside the circle of their natural comfort that they are likely to grow.

When an organization is weak on customer service and is trying to build its strength in that area, it is useful to say that it is trying to reconfigure itself along the lines of an extraverted feeling character—outwardly oriented and concerned with people. Individuals in the typological categories of ESFJ, ENFJ, ESFP, and ENFP can greatly strengthen that effort. Another organization that is just emerging from the venture stage and needs to systematize its activities would find ISTJs and ISFJs to be especially valuable.

These typical intersections of organizational need and individual resource can be approached from either the organizational side—in which case they fall under the heading of staffing strategies—or from the individual side—in which case they form part of career development. In either case, they involve meshing type and character in a way that would be impossible using the MBTI alone.

In the end, career development involves a kind of *triangulation*, in which an individual's personal type, the normative type of a career field, and the character of the organization for which he or she works need to be in at least some degree of harmony. Once again, remember that absolute identity of types and character is neither necessary nor even advantageous. Absolute identity would feel a little dull to all but the most security-oriented people, and it certainly wouldn't stretch the person nor help to develop the organization much. The goal to aim at is a positive and creative tension in the triangular pattern.

Character and Team Building

On the smaller scale of a work team, the same kind of coordination between character and type is useful. Here it comes under the heading of team building. As we consider the character of the team, we need to remember that the character of any group is not just the sum total of the individual temperaments in it, for it is also greatly influenced by the leader's typology and the character of that particular functional activity that the team engages in.

I once worked with the controller's office of a large corporation in which the individual typologies within the management team were heavily weighted toward feeling. This surprising fact—which was the product of historical accident—would have led one to define feeling as the dominant team characteristic. But that was not so. In fact the feeling function, though numerically in the majority, did not fit the team in many ways. The reason was in the character of that particular organization: Its accounting and regulatory function was sensing and thinking, and its new leader was an INTJ.

The team building task with that particular group was only partly to get the staff to understand the typology of its new leader and vice versa—which was the part of the task based on the MBTI results. It was also to work to develop the character of the organization in such a way that the individuals had a comfortable and useful place in it. You cannot change an individual's type, and so the director's influence was a given (although educating him to the characteristic pitfalls of his type helped a good deal). The most useful intervention was to help the group redefine their business in a way that gave it a different and more comfortable character, one that permitted team members a more legitimate way to express their natural feeling.

It happened that the director had arrived with an idea that he wanted to try. (INTJs often have terrific ideas that they want to try.) He suggested that the controller's office should be in the business, not of enforcing financial rules, but of providing regulatory services. Feeling types are usually not very good *enforcers*, but they are great as *service providers*. As the team regrouped around this redefinition of their mission and worked out the functional and structural implications of that redefinition, they came together as a new and much stronger team.

In this day when work is so important to most people's identities, *the team* is at least the second most important *other* in their lives. Where personal relationships and family life are not central to an individual, the team in which they work is usually the most important other. There is no way to work on such an important relationship unless one has a way of characterizing this other and then rebuilding the relationship with it to be more comfortable and workable. As the case of the controller's office shows, that is only partly accomplished interpersonally—between the individual and others as individuals. It also requires a modification or development of the relation between the organizational character and personal type.

Using Character and Type to Ease Career Transitions

There is an additional way that type and character can be used together, and that is as a way of informing an individual about the environment that he or she is about to enter through employment, transfer, or promotion. When people arrive for a new assignment in an organization in which they have never before worked, they often waste valuable time trying to figure out the expectations that await them. Often these expectations are somewhat unconscious to those that hold them, so that direct questions (even if an employee is brave enough to ask) do not necessarily provide accurate or useful information.

To be able to provide such an employee with a character profile of his or her new organization can save valuable time. And if the profile is supplemented with a little education about how an individual of that employee's particular type tends to misunderstand or be misunderstood by an organization of that particular character, the odds of successful assimilation go up considerably.

But one need not stop there. The management of the group the employee is entering ought to have information about the character of its own organization. Armed with that information and understanding better their own weaknesses and blindnesses, management can communicate more effectively with individuals who are birds of a different feather. Such communications will do a great deal to ease the new employee's transition. A final step in this process is to design an *incorporation session*, in which the person and representatives of the organization meet and talk through their type- and character-based differences in assumptions and expectations.

This is particularly important when the new individual in question is the organization's new leader. Since that person may have been chosen expressly to compensate for organizational characteristics (see below for a discussion of compensatory leadership), he or she is not only an outsider but also something of an alien. A careful study and discussion of areas of similarity and difference, in this case, should definitely be supplemented by a carefully planned meeting in which each party in the new relationship has a chance to spell out what it can give to the other, as well as its needs from the other.

Character and Leadership

Taken out of context, "Character and Leadership" sounds as though it might deal with the characteristics that successful leaders share with one another. We've had more than enough of such books: In the first place, the number of generalizations you can make about the enormous variety of men and women who have been successful leaders is really fairly small and rather uninteresting. In the second place, it obscures and diverts attention from an important truth that a leader is right for a particular organization at a particular time only if there is a characterological fit between them.

Most people would agree that Lee Iacocca, Joan of Arc, Mahatma Ghandi, Martin Luther King, Jr., and Maggie Thatcher were all strong leaders. With some ingenuity, we could extract a list of common traits that they shared—although the more you know about any of them as an individual, the more doubts you are sure to have about the list. The irony is that the one thing that they undeniably have in common will not even be on the list: that is, that each was the right person to lead a particular organization, society, or movement at that particular time.

The implications of that last sentence are complex and could easily fill a book of their own.[3] This is not that book, so my present concern is only to lay out a way of looking at the relation between the character of an organization and what is needed to lead that organization at a particular time in its development. To do that, we need to begin by distinguishing between two different relations that a leader can have to the characterological tendencies of his or her organization. She or he can *represent* those tendencies or can *compensate* for them.

The Representative Leader

Representative leaders express the natural character of their organizations. If their organization is extraverted, they are extraverted. If it emphasizes thinking over feeling, they do too. Representative leaders are most successful during two different times in the organization's life.

The first is when things are fairly stable and the organization's intrinsic character fits with the internal and external situation it is facing. The leader's job at such times is to focus the organization's efforts and its resources in familiar ways, according to familiar priorities. To say that such a leader is a *traditional* leader would be misleading, because the tradition of that particular organization could be to innovate rather than to preserve the traditional ways of doing things. But even in such a situation, the representative leader embodies an organizational identity that does not have to change much.

The second time that the representative leader can be very important is when the organization has drifted away from the activities or the policies that are native to its intrinsic character—either by pursuing opportunities or by trying to resist threats. At such a time, a representative leader may be the right person to call the organization back to its characteristic areas of strength. Again, to say that this leader's job is to espouse tradition is misleading, for he or she may not only be recalling a heritage of innovation but may also be calling on people to make a painful break with a recent past during which the organization strayed from its characteristic path. As in the first instance, however, representative leaders mirror the native character of their organization in their outlook and style. And in each case, representative leaders express the symbolic continuities in their organizations.

The Problem With Representative Leaders

When significant organizational changes are called for, representative leaders can make them only if they do not require the organization to work across the grain of its natural character. A company in a volatile industry may have, let's say, an ENTP character. Such a character—which is common among young, fast-moving organizations in the venture phase of their development—makes it responsive to external changes, forward looking, and logical in its responses. And such a character makes it able and willing to change to take advantage of opportunities.

But let's imagine that it grows significantly and begins to differentiate its work force into large departments made up of more specialized employees. Some of these newer employees are more security oriented than those who joined the company when it was smaller. Having less knowledge of or contact with the leadership, they are more easily distressed and disoriented by changes than the original employees were. The ENTP character frightens them, with its relative disinterest in the human dimension of organizational situations. The organization begins to have morale problems, and there is a growing mistrust of the leadership. The organization's characteristic weakness in the area of feeling is starting to become a problem.

At the same time, the growth may overload the unsystematized policy-making and information-handling resources of the organization. The old shoot-from-the-hip style of making decisions and the back-of-the-envelope style of keeping records is no longer sufficient to handle the complex environment that the organization is facing. Its deficiency in the areas of sensing and judging is starting to cause serious problems.

And finally, there is the problem of extraversion. The current (and representative) leadership keeps demanding that everyone focus on the external environment. It does so in the name of customer service and competitiveness—both of which are qualities no one can argue with. But internally there are the growing morale and system problems we have just described. The ENTP character is not only slow to become aware of such problems, but it also underestimates their significance once they have been identified. The ENTP organization reacts to the expression of concern for these things with impatience.[4] It is also likely to idealize the good old days when "we all worked fourteen hour days and there wasn't this damned belly aching all the time!"

The Compensatory Leader

An organization like the one described above has come to a critical point in its developmental path. Its inherent organizational character has become a problem, and leadership that simply represents that character is going to become a debit. What is needed is a leader or a leadership group that compensates in specific ways for the shortcomings of the organization's inherent character. In this particular case, the leader needs to have more feeling and a more highly developed introversion.

As far as the need for stronger doses of sensing and judging, they can probably be supplied by executives or managers at the next level down from the top. It is at their level that effective systems and formal policies have to be developed and implemented. The top leader needs to understand and appreciate the need for such things, but he or she does not have to do the job personally.

Now, what I am recommending does not mean that you have to give all candidates for the job of president the MBTI and look for an ISFJ type. It simply means that whoever is chosen cannot be a representative leader and that he or she needs more highly developed introversion and feeling than the old leader had.[5] It also means that whoever is chosen needs to understand the character-based needs of the organization at this point and to be able to act on that understanding.

That may mean selecting assistants or advisors who compensate for the organization's and perhaps the leader's own weaknesses. It may mean a development program designed to strengthen the introverted and feeling tendencies in the leadership team generally, both through an infusion of new blood and through education of the old members. It may mean establishing policies that serve to remind team members of the things that they tend to overlook or forget.

The Problem With Compensatory Leaders

While compensatory leaders are critically important to an organization's development and long-term survival, they are no panacea. In the first place, they are only appropriate when the organization needs to change its characteristic way of operating. To bring them in often would be to doom the organization to a succession of changes that would not add up to any consistent direction and would, instead, leave it tacking back and forth in a way that slowed it down considerably.

In the second place, compensatory leaders represent a serious challenge to the organizational system, and so they need to be saved for when they are really needed. They often undertake "housecleaning" efforts that involve replacing people who have been with the organization for a long time. That may be necessary, but it is heroic medicine that cannot be repeated often.

The third problem with the compensatory leader is that he or she may be insensitive to the character of the organization and, therefore, very ineffective in communicating. No matter how uncharacteristic the action that one must take, some tie needs to be found to the organization's characteristic assumptions or outlook or value system.

Representative and compensatory leaders will equally qualify as "great" if they are at the right place at the right time. Both Washington and Lincoln were representative in many ways, and they represented those aspects of the American character that were needed in their particular situation. And both Jackson and Franklin Roosevelt were compensatory, the former being a counterweight to the elitist groups that had run things since the Revolution and the latter being a counterweight to the business interests that had run things since the Civil War. Both of them turned the characteristic tide of affairs at a time when that tide had gone as far as it could constructively.

Type and Character for Change Agents

Throughout this chapter, I have been discussing how to use the relationships between type and character to improve the organization's functioning through career development, team building, and leadership selection. In so doing, I have bypassed one very important type/character issue: the type of the person who is trying to improve the organization's functioning. Unless that person is aware of the way in which his or her own type corresponds to or contrasts with the character of the organization in question, serious mistakes can be made.

In the first place, the very notion of change agent is typologically loaded. Most people who would identify themselves in those terms are intuitives, either charismatic NFs or innovative NTs. Such people have a great deal to bring to sensing organizations, but they have some of the same shortcomings that compensatory leaders do. That is, they will never succeed in capitalizing on their gifts unless they understand what the character is that they are trying to change and how their efforts need to be explained to an organization of that character.

Understanding the relation between the organization's character and their own particular type helps change agents in three ways. First, it enables them to understand why a particular change is going to be so difficult for a particular organization. Most organizational development is, after all, nothing less than an effort at real character change, and it needs to be seen in that light. Armed with this insight, the change agent is less likely to underestimate the time and resources necessary to make the change.

Second, understanding the character of the organization one is trying to change enables one to tailor change strategies to capitalize on its strengths and avoid as much as possible efforts that would rely on its weak suits. Finally, understanding character makes one much more conscious of one's own type-based limitations. Doing to others as one would be done to is fine ethics, but it is often not very good human relations, since it is based on the mistaken idea that "the other" is essentially like oneself: An extravert thrives on the socializing that wears an introvert out. The thinker prefers the same rather impersonal decision-making process that drives the feeling type up the wall.

The first thing that the change agent needs to do is to understand as much as he or she can about the unique way that his or her own personal type sees the world and prefers to operate in it. Unless the change agent becomes conscious of those things, he or she will consider such ways of going at things to be simply normal and assume that the organization shares them. Reading all that you can about your individual type and even discussing with a counselor how it colors your experience and shapes your assumptions is the very important first step.

The second thing that the change agent needs to do is to establish the character of his or her organizational client. Having done that, the change agent must get inside that character and understand from inside out how it influences the organization's view of the world and of itself.

- What does it mean, for example, that the sensing organization prefers changes that improve or vary the status quo but do not alter it in any fundamental way? How will that outlook shape the way the organization perceives and judges the reorganization that one is going to be working on?

- What does it mean that a thinking organization prefers to use general principles to judge situations and that it instinctively distrusts conclusions that spring from individual convictions and personal value systems? (One thing it certainly means is that the change agent, an intuitive–feeling type who likes to talk about organizational transformation, is going to have to do some translating to adapt his or her views into something that the client can buy.)

Change agents must reframe their message to fit the client's character-based frame of reference. If the client is introverted, it might be useful to go back and find a tie between these new ideas and the founder's original intent or actions. When Roger Smith launched his change attempts at General Motors, he tried to do this by saying that what he was doing was just what that corporation's early, great CEO, William Durant, would have done if he had been leading the organization. If the client is extraverted, it would probably work better to tell of the use of one's ideas by other, visibly successful companies. "When Hewlett-Packard faced this kind of a situation...the successful customer-service effort at SAS was based on...Ford lowered defects from 13% to .05% by...."

Change agents must also adapt their strategies to the strengths and weaknesses of the client's character, not to those of some ideal client. If teamwork is difficult and individual effort is the natural form taken by human activity in an organization, it makes more sense to design an intervention that spotlights individual effort and creates teamwork indirectly than it does to offer an organizational recipe that begins, "Take a smoothly functioning team, and...." If introversion and thinking make written communication the normal form of communication in an organization, the change agent needs to forget the plan for the big meeting where the CEO paints the picture of the future in an impromptu, heart-felt speech. A written communication in which the CEO is helped to talk as personally as possible about his or her plans is a better first step.

Individual Type and Organizational Character—A Reprise

In career planning, team building, leadership development, and change agentry, being able to identify and understand the implications of an organization's character allows one either to reinforce its strengths or to balance its weaknesses with organizational development interventions or with the addition of individuals of a given type. In the latter case, it makes it possible to help the individual select or get ready to enter an organization successfully.

But matching the organization and the individual must be done with caution. Neither the *Myers-Briggs Type Indicator* nor the *Organizational Character Index* should be used as a screening device. Even leaving aside legal issues—though those alone make employment decisions based on type testing very dangerous—a decision based on MBTI and OCI results alone would not necessarily be a good one.

Both on the organizational and on the individual sides of the issue, matching a person with a place on the organization chart involves much more than simply meshing character and type. It also involves assuring that there is a fit between individual abilities and organizational role demands, as well as a fit between personal goals and organizational purposes. Further, a successful match requires that everyone be clear on whether the organization needs someone who reflects its already existing character or someone who will help to balance it with other type qualities. And the latter will often be the case, for if everyone is simply a clone of the organization there will be no one to turn the tide of lemmings to the sea.

Nor am I, in touting the uses of organizational character, suggesting that other ways of matching individuals and positions be abandoned. I am just pointing out that the ordinary ways of thinking about the fit between person and job or change agent and organization have a serious flaw: They lack a reliable technique for matching the individual and the organizational personalities. That lack is as damaging as would be an approach to marriage that was based on the assurance that the couple possessed congruent skills and similar motivations, but that lacked any data about whether the two people were emotionally compatible.

Chapter Seven

Character and Destiny

Although changing an organization's character is certainly possible, it is difficult and takes more time and resources than organizations usually provide. That is why one so often finds that after all the big transformative changes have been made, the organization is still disappointingly unchanged in some very important ways. One can either look at that with discouragement or see it as a sign that organizations have natural paths that they must follow. While there is nothing fixed about it, it is possible to feel that Heraclitus was right when he said 2,500 years ago, "Character is destiny."

Heraclitus certainly did not mean that all the events of the future are enfolded into the moment of individual or organizational birth. He simply meant that, for all of the variations that there are among oak trees, all acorns *do* grow into oaks. None grow into buzzards or shrimp. All creatures remain bounded by their limitations and possibilities, even if some of those possibilities are to transcend what appear at some point to be their limitations.

I believe that character *is* destiny, though not in a narrowly restrictive sense. Hundreds of thousands of individuals who have taken the MBTI or other type tests and have seen their characteristics described in the results have found themselves strengthened by the knowledge. "There!" they say. "That *is* who I am!" Learning of their typological strengths, they feel empowered and as though they are on track at last. Learning of their typological weaknesses, they feel alerted to, but not blamed or judged for, pitfalls that they dimly knew were there but were never before able to identify—and so unable to avoid.

In understanding both their strengths and weaknesses, they become better equipped to do what they can do. What they do feels in some way right. It becomes *easy* in the sense that any natural action is easier than an unnatural one. It feels, somehow, *destined*, and destiny feels like a friend rather than an enemy.

Discovering the character of an organization or an institution has the same effect. "That's us," we say. "That *is* what we're good at!" Or, "No wonder we have trouble with marketing or product development or customer relations or financial management." Like an individual, the organization is what it is, and it does its best when it operates in harmony with that identity. Self-knowledge is validating and strengthening.

This is not to say that difficulty with marketing or with anything else is an excuse for not doing it. It is simply to say that the difficult activity is going to take longer, require more care, and be more frustrating than it would be for an organization with a character that was more in line with the activity. And it is to say that the difficulty is not a blameworthy condition. It is like shyness or dreaminess or literalness or any other personal characteristic: something to accept and balance with characteristic strengths.

There are really only four ways to deal wisely with whatever strengths and weaknesses an organization has:

- Avoiding its weaknesses: An organization can try to stay out of projects and businesses that place a premium on what the organization doesn't naturally do very well.

- Compensating for its weaknesses: An organization can find external resources—an acquisition, a joint venture partner, a new group of employees, or a compensatory leader—to offset the characteristic organizational weakness.

- Developing new strengths: An organization can use the organizational development tactics that we discussed earlier to develop its shadow side.

- Capitalizing on its existing strengths: An organization must find ways of concentrating its resources on products or services that go with the characterological grain instead of against it.

The trouble is that these common-sense strategies for organizational enhancement are seldom undertaken with any understanding of organizational character.

- *An extraverted–sensing organization* is resisting a new career development program that it badly needs. It would deal with the situation better if it understood the importance of organizational character and could see itself as trying to develop the appreciation for its own inner resources and processes that is more characteristic of an introverted organization and of people's potentials, the way intuitive organizations do.

- *A thinking organization* is trying to figure out how to deal with its morale problems and how to get employees to buy into difficult changes that have to be made if the organization is going to survive. Instead of simply explaining things again, such an organization needs to begin by understanding the limitations of the thinking character and to see that it is trying to develop the concern for people that is more natural to a feeling organization.

- *An introverted–intuitive organization* that wants to capitalize on a terrific new product that it has invented needs to consider whether it should develop the sensing qualities needed to manufacture it and the extraverted ones needed to market it, or whether an acquisition of or joint venture with a small extraverted–sensing manufacturing firm is the better path.

In each case, it is character that provides the key to what needs to be done. And it is character that provides the key to how to frame and present the plan in terms that the particular organization at that time in its developmental cycle can accept.

The Organizational Character Index

I think that the best way to establish the character of any organizational entity is to get a group of representatives from that entity together, teach them about the four different spectra of organizational character, and then have them talk it out: "Push for closure? Hell, we're a steam roller!" says one. "A 'J' organization if there ever was one." Or: "Extraverted? Get serious! We've never asked a customer for any reaction to what we do. Instead, the executives sit up in their board room and create our policies and strategy out of their heads!" Out of such give-and-take, a picture begins to emerge.

But that takes time, and it is difficult to involve more than a few people in the undertaking. That is why I have developed an index that can be used to poll a wider audience and to do so more quickly. Its advantage is that you can give it to people who do not know anything about organizational character—in fact, ignorance of the subject insures an element of objectivity—and in 15 minutes have their assessment of the organization. You can do this with 50 people and get a sample that would be impossible to get in any discussion group.

There are, of course, disadvantages to depending on the *Organizational Character Index*—or OCI, as we shall call it. Here are some of them:

- Questions can be interpreted differently by people who lack the chance to discuss them and who do not understand the concepts behind them. If you use the OCI, be sure that the people who take it understand the questions.

- Some people answer the questions in terms of the real organization that operates every day, while others answer the question in terms of the organization that its leaders describe. *Is* and *ought to be* are different organizations, as are *presently is* and *is trying to become*. People should answer the questions in terms of actuality, not professed ideals.

- Everyone inevitably characterizes the organization that he or she has personally experienced. (When this is done by an isolated individual with a piece of paper, that subjectivity may not be as clear as it is when issues are discussed in a group.) So, don't depend on one person's ratings—even yours. A group as small as ten can compensate for this individual angle of vision. Further, discussion within the group will serve to remind people that their individual experience may not be representative, so it is useful to include such discussion in the process of administering the index.

- And finally, the OCI has not been statistically validated. It is simply the current best tool for inventorying the character-related qualities of an organization. As I said in the preface, I hope that this book leads to the kinds of studies that need to be undertaken if its validity and reliability are to be established.

All those problems not withstanding, the OCI is a useful tool.

Unlike the MBTI and other personal type instruments, the OCI allows people to register the degree or strength of choice between the two opposites. Using a four-point scale, it allows one to go beyond "A" or "B":

1 = Distinctly (or usually) A
2 = Somewhat (or often) A
3 = Somewhat (or often) B
4 = Distinctly (or usually) B

It does force people to come down on one side or the other of the middle point, however.

Anyone who takes it should not agonize too much about his or her answers. If in doubt, go with the first thought you had when you read the question. And remember: Leave no questions blank.

Question	Rating			
1. Does the organization pay more attention to the demands of its customers or to what it knows how to do best?	Customers			What it does best
	1	2	3	4
2. Is the organization better at producing and delivering established products/services or at planning or creating new ones?	Producing/ delivering			Planning/ creating
	1	2	3	4
3. Which is more important to the organization: its efficient systems or its dedicated people?	Systems			People
	1	2	3	4
4. Does the organization spell out the details of its policies and procedures, or does it avoid such detail in the name of letting people work in their own best style?	Spell out			Avoid too much detail
	1	2	3	4
5. Can employees see the organization's inner workings fairly clearly, or is decision making invisible to most people—with decisions simply appearing mysteriously?	Very open			Very hidden
	1	2	3	4
6. Does the leadership base its decisions on detailed information about situations or on general trends and a big picture or concept of what is going on?	Detailed information			Big picture
	1	2	3	4
7. Does the organization ask of people that they fill their official roles effectively or that they exercise their individual talents fully?	Official roles			Individual talent
	1	2	3	4
8. Would you say that the organization emphasizes reaching a decision quickly or considering things from every angle, even if it takes quite a while?	Decisions			Look at every angle
	1	2	3	4

Question	Rating			

9. Are decisions more often made because of market data or because of internal factors like the beliefs of the leaders or the capacities of the facilities?

	Market data			Internal factors
	1	2	3	4

10. Does the organization more often steer its course by the actualities of the present situation or by the possibilities it perceives in the future?

	Actualities			Possibilities
	1	2	3	4

11. How are organizational decisions really made—with the head (tempered by humanity) or the heart (balanced by information)?

	Tempered head			Balanced heart
	1	2	3	4

12. If the organization has a fault, is it that it locks into decisions too quickly or that it keeps too many options open for too long?

	Too quickly			Too many options
	1	2	3	4

13. Do the organization's people and component units collaborate naturally and from the beginning of a project or somewhat uncomfortably and after their separate positions have been established?

	From the beginning			After the fact
	1	2	3	4

14. When changes are being discussed, which gets more attention—the step-by-step plan for getting to the destination or the vision of where things are going?

	Steps			Vision
	1	2	3	4

15. Which are taken more seriously in dealing with personnel issues—general principles and standards or individual circumstances and situations?

	Principles			Circumstances
	1	2	3	4

16. Does the organization more often act on the basis of set priorities or because of opportunities it discovers in its external environment?

	Priorities			Opportunities
	1	2	3	4

Question	Rating			
17. Is it the influence of competitors, regulators, and customers or its own sense of its identity and mission that is more likely to dictate the organization's actions?	Relations 1	2	3	Identity/ mission 4
18. Is the organization better at producing reliable products and data or at coming up with innovative ideas or designs?	Reliable products 1	2	3	Innovative ideas 4
19. At the organization, does *communicating* mean giving information to or staying in touch with its constituencies?	Giving information 1	2	3	Staying in touch 4
20. Does the organization rely on carefully established procedures or on "playing it as it lays"?	Procedures 1	2	3	"As it lays" 4
21. Which usually determines the organization's direction—the external challenges it faces or the internal resources it possesses?	Challenges 1	2	3	Resources 4
22. Is the organization's leadership better described as *solid* and *down to earth* or as *intuitive* and *visionary*?	Down to earth 1	2	3	Visionary 4
23. Which more accurately describes the way managers are supposed to act—following rational policies or acting sensitively and humanely?	Rational policies 1	2	3	Sensitive and humane 4
24. Does the organization more often choose to reach a decision or look for more options?	Decide 1	2	3	Look for more options 4
25. Is the organization fairly open to influence by employees, customers, or even the public, or is it a pretty tightly closed system?	Open 1	2	3	Closed 4

Question	Rating			

26. Do the organization's values emphasize acting practically and reliably or ingenuously and inventively?	Practically I	2	3	Ingeniously 4
27. When people in the organization talk about "the right thing to do," are they referring to the logical and rational thing or the humane and sensitive thing?	Logical/ rational I	2	3	Humane/ sensitive 4
28. Which better describes the organization's style—stick to solid ground or ride the river of change?	Solid ground I	2	3	River of change 4
29. In terms of strategy, is the organization driven by its clients' needs and its competitors' actions, or by its functional and professional capabilities?	Client/ competitor I	2	3	Functional/ professional 4
30. When big changes must be made, does the organization prefer to deal with them incrementally (broken down into little steps) or holistically (as one integrated transformational leap)?	Incrementally I	2	3	Holistically 4
31. Is the organization better described as a structure of task-based positions (where the relationships are secondary) or a system in which relationships are almost as important as tasks?	Task- based I	2	3	Relationship- based 4
32. When projects are being planned, are they usually tightly scheduled on a fixed timetable, or flexibly scheduled on an itinerary that can change with circumstances?	Tightly scheduled I	2	3	Flexibly scheduled 4

Question	Rating			
33. Does the organization work well with suppliers, joint venture partners, and professional associations, or does it prefer to go it alone?	Works with others I	2	3	Goes it alone 4
34. Which better describes the organization—sticking to the tried and true or undertaking bold new ventures?	Tried and true I	2	3	Bold new ventures 4
35. Which better describes the leader(s)' style—criticism or encouragement?	Criticism I	2	Encouragement 3	4
36. Is the organization more likely to plan ahead, or make it up as it goes along?	Plan ahead I	2	3	Make it up as it goes 4

When you have finished the OCI, put the numerical ratings you selected for each of the 36 questions in the spaces after those numbers below. Then add up the numbers in each horizontal line and enter the totals to the right; then convert your total to a letter according to the directions (e.g., 22 or less is an E, 23 or more is an I).

1 __ 5 __ 9 __ 13 __ 17 __ 21 __ 25 __ 29 __ 33 __ Total ____ [22 = E; 23 = I]

2 __ 6 __ 10 __ 14 __ 18 __ 22 __ 26 __ 30 __ 34 __ Total ____ [22 = S; 23 = N]

3 __ 7 __ 11 __ 15 __ 19 __ 23 __ 27 __ 31 __ 35 __ Total ____ [22 = T; 23 = F]

4 __ 8 __ 12 __ 16 __ 20 __ 24 __ 28 __ 32 __ 36 __ Total ____ [22 = J; 23 = P]

According to the *Organizational Character Index*, your organization's character is ☐☐☐☐

This code may be the same as the one you came up with back at the end of chapter 2, or it may be slightly different. However you determine an organization's character, you ought to supplement your own evaluations with others' to balance any limited perspective or personal bias that you may have.

Appendix B

Bibliographical Notes

The best material on organizational character is not about organizations at all, but about individuals and the psychology of type differences. The seminal book on that subject is C. G. Jung's *Psychological Types* (1923), but if nothing else had been written on the subject, not many people would appreciate its importance. For all its historical importance, Jung's book is less interesting than books that came after it.

The Myers-Briggs work is summarized in Isabel Briggs Myers' *Gifts Differing* (1990, 1980), the "bible" of the modern-day study of psychological type. An independent but related line of work has been carried on by David Keirsey, and his findings are summarized in two books: *Please Understand Me: Character and Temperament Types* (1984) and *Portraits of Temperament* (1987). Two recent books that synthesize all of these approaches are Otto Kroeger and Janet M. Thuesen, *Type Talk* (1988) and Sandra Hirsh and Jean Kummerow, *LifeTypes* (1989).

Hirsh and Kummerow have also written about the uses of individual typology in an organizational setting. Their pamphlet is called *Introduction to Type in Organizations* (1987). Hirsh has also created a resource notebook entitled *Using the Myers-Briggs Type Indicator in Organizations* (1985). Another book on type in a work setting is *Working Together* (1988) by Olaf Isachsen and Linda Berens.

One of the few interesting attempts to use Jungian typology to actually describe organizations will be found in "The Manager's Personality as Stakeholder" in Ian I. Mitroff's *Stakeholders of the Organizational Mind* (1983).

Character and Culture

It has become fashionable to ascribe many of the differences among organizations to differences in the organizations' cultures. *Culture* has various definitions, but it is usually said to involve the values and beliefs that are widely shared within an organization. Students of organizational culture are particularly interested in the ceremonies, symbols, and legends that are current within a company or institution, since anthropologists have generally maintained that a culture is more clearly expressed in the organization's relatively unconscious gestures and artifacts than in its official policies and pronouncements. These aspects of culture are notoriously hard to pin down, however, and there is no generally agreed-upon way to inventory an organization's culture. The result is that culture studies must generally fall back on impressionistic and subjective interpretations of people's words and actions.

There's another problem with using culture to explain the differences in style and temperament among organizations. Although anthropologists are still debating the meaning of culture among themselves, you would seldom realize that fact to hear the term used by organizational speakers and writers who talk confidently about "the IBM culture" and "the culture of General Motors." Like many who borrow concepts from other fields, organizational writers have oversimplified matters to such an extent that their concept has lost much of its connection to the usages that are current in the field to which it belongs.

Another problem is that the anthropological concept of culture is only really useful in describing patterns that have developed slowly and unconsciously over a period of generations. It is misleading to use the term to describe the new value system that the CEO picked up from the book he or she just read or that the organizational development group fell in love with during that seminar they attended last weekend. Yet those concepts—like participative management, quality improvement, and entrapreneurship—are the very value-clusters that become the core of the "culture change" efforts that so many organizations are undertaking these days.

The tribe that the anthropologist studies does not change its culture self-consciously just because somebody decides that a new and better culture exists among a tribe on a neighboring island. Neither, for that matter, does an organization—although one wouldn't guess that fact from the debates that occur about cultures of excellence or customer service. An organization's culture changes very, very slowly over a period of years, partly through intentional interventions but largely through the sum total of people's only partly articulated responses to a changing world or marketplace.

The idea of *organizational culture* is, therefore, one that raises as many problems as it solves. This book has been written in the belief that there is a more reliable and readily identifiable concept than culture to use in discussing why organizations behave the way they do: that is the organization's character.

Notes

Chapter One

1. See chapter 3 for descriptions of these sixteen basic categories.

2. These scales represent relative tendencies, not absolute characteristics, and most organizations show some mixture of the two qualities in question. But—and here is what makes "character" assessable—one predominates and its relative strength can be measured.

3. "Can UPS Deliver the Goods in a New World?" *Business Week*, June 4, 1990, pp. 80 ff.

4. These four-letter designations will be used throughout the book. MBTI devotees will be familiar with them, and others will learn to use them quickly.

5. This does not necessarily mean that the individuals in the two departments are, respectively, extraverts and introverts—although they often are.

6. Much that we say will also be true of social groupings, like families, communities, cultural or ethnic groups, and nations, but those groupings are not organizations as we are using the term, and they are not our subject here.

7. In the case of a multinational corporation, the branch in a particular country may be so strongly influenced by the local culture that it shares more characteristics with the local branches of other multinationals than it does with its own home office. For a study of the disparate value systems within multinational corporations, see André Laurent, "The Cross-Cultural Puzzle of International Human Resource Management," *Human Resource Management*, Spring, 1986, pp. 91–102.

8. "Man or woman," I'd like to add. But then, I'd like to say that in spite of exceptions like Liz Claiborne, Mrs. Fields Cookies, and the Sisters of Charity,

most organizations are founded by men. No wonder so many organizations are thinking in their character, for so are six out of ten men.

9. Be careful not to make thoughtless generalizations about all companies in a given business, however. The following statement from a company manual bespeaks a feeling orientation rather than a thinking one, even though its business (electronic equipment) is dominated by thinking companies: "While acknowledging the necessity for policies, procedures, and basic management control systems, we attempt to hold these to a minimum and invest more effort in developing sound human judgment. This reflects our belief that individual judgment is generally more reliable than rules and regulations." The company in question is Analog Devices. The quote comes from Robert Levering's *The 100 Best Companies to Work for in America* (New York: Signet, 1987), p. 6.

10. Among writers on psychological type, the combinations of intuition–feeling or intuition–thinking are called the person's *temperament*. So are sensing–thinking and sensing–feeling—or in the case of David Keirsey and his followers, sensing–judging or sensing–perceiving. It is useful to be able to group the sixteen types into four general categories like this, and I will occasionally do that in this book.

11. See chapter 4, "Character, Growth, and Change," where the stages of organizational life are discussed more systematically.

Chapter Two

1. Quoted by Frank Rose, "Now Quality Means Service Too," *Fortune* (April 22, 1991), p. 100.

2. Electronic mail, incidentally, has been a boon to introverted organizations because it has allowed them to gain some of the benefits of extraversion with little of the "messiness" of conversation.

3. In my work with two very successful electronics companies, an introverted one and an extraverted one, I've observed that the introverted company is loathe to bring an outsider in: "What can he know about us? He'll just impose his own ideas on us." The extraverted company, too, has its doubts about using my transition management services. But they are different doubts: "That 'human relations' stuff will distract us from what we need to do, which is to gain market share. Let's use our money for marketing, not management development." It's important to recognize that there isn't any character without its characteristic biases and blind spots. The important thing is to understand them and take them into account.

4. In the terminology of psychological type, *feeling* does not mean *emotion*, but rather refers to a value-driven, personally based way of reaching judgments and decisions. Nonetheless, organizations with a well-developed feeling character are usually more tolerant of emotion than those where feeling is less developed.

5. Ironically, since they so systematically overlook feeling, it is thinking organizations where there may be more rage and bitterness to spill over.

6. In response to the criticism that he was too hard on people, TWA's Carl Icahn is reported to have said, "If I'd wanted to be loved, I'd have got a dog."

7. From Richard Tanner Pascale, *Managing on the Edge*, New York: Simon and Schuster, 1990, p. 226.

8. A famous (but admittedly extreme) example of a perceiving organization was Atari, the computer and computer-game company founded by the decidedly perceiving type Nolan Bushnell. According to an article written by David Sheff, "employees worked when they wanted to, staff meetings were rare, and the founder wore T-shirts or flowery shirts with polka-dot ties. As Steve Jobs, one of Atari's early employees, remembers, 'The smell of marijuana ran freely through the air-conditioning system. Rock and roll played out on the production floor....' [Another colleague of Bushnell's adds:] 'Nolan's enthusiasm is infectious. It just doesn't last.... His attention span is about as long as the number of projects he's working on.'" From "Reversal of Fortune," *San Francisco Focus Magazine*, May 1991, pp. 54 ff.

Chapter Three

1. If you took the OCI (Appendix A) and one of the scores was borderline (17 or 18), you should also read the description of what it would have been had the score been just one point higher or lower.

Chapter Four

1. For a fuller discussion of the organizational life cycle and its phases, see "Turning Points in the Organizational Life Cycle," in my book, *Surviving Organizational Transition* (Mill Valley, CA: William Bridges & Associates, 1990), pp. 97–118.

2. *Inc.* magazine regularly runs a column on such entrepreneurial ideas—with critiques of them by a panel of experts.

3. Writing the four-letter code with a blank in it means that that space in the code—in this case, the T or the F—is not relevant to the point we are making. It could be INTP or INFP. And the code given in the next paragraph could be either ESFJ or ESTJ.

4. See my books, *Transitions: Making Sense of Life's Changes* (Reading, MA: Addison-Wesley, 1980) for a discussion of this process in a personal setting, and *Surviving Corporate Transition* (Mill Valley, CA: William Bridges & Associates, 1990) and *Managing Transitions* (Reading, MA: Addison-Wesley, 1991) for a discussion of it in an organizational setting.

Chapter Five

1. See Subrata N. Chakravarty, "We Had to Change the Playing Field," *Forbes*, February 4, 1991, p. 83.

2. If you want a generic description of your organizational shadow, reverse each of the letters in your character-designation: turn an E into an I (or vice versa), an S to an N, etc. Then take this characterological mirror image of your organization and go back to chapter 3 and read a description of it. It will be the character type that your own organization would have the most trouble understanding or working closely with. (In actuality, most of the organizations that you work with would be unlikely to be the complete opposite. They would probably differ in only a couple of key aspects. But exaggerating differences can illustrate the point effectively.)

3. It is important to note here that we are not talking about simply misunderstanding the environment—which can come from misinformation or from the lack of a meaningful context in which to view it. And we are not talking about wishful thinking, which may lead to underestimating threats or overestimating resources. We are rather talking about a psychologically based distortion of the perceptual field, wherein an organization fails to see other organizations realistically because it endows them with the very qualities and characteristics which it has failed to find or develop in itself.

4. From Leonard Sayles, "The Success Problem," *Boardroom Reports*, Jan. 1, 1991, p. 2.

5. McGraw-Hill has recently been suffering from its failure to make such distinctions. Its CEO became enamored of a concept and tried to remake the company around it. He failed. *Forbes* recently detailed the damage in an article subtitled, "A Publishing Company Is Not an Information Turbine." It cost McGraw-Hill $172 million to find that out. See Suzanne L. Oliver's "Management by Concept" in the magazine's November 26, 1990, issue, pp. 37–38.

6. In their book, *Type Talk* (New York: Dell, 1988), Otto Kroeger and Janet Thuesen suggest that it was the preponderance of judging types at NASA that made it difficult for the agency to abandon its scheduled Challenger flight, even though some of the engineers believed that there were problems with it.

7. From John Sculley, *Odyssey: Pepsi to Apple*, New York: Harper & Row, 1987, p. 128.

8. For a detailed description of BP's redevelopment project, see D. Quinn Mills, *Rebirth of the Corporation*, New York: Wiley, 1991, pp. 91–107. Quinn's book as a whole can be read as a guide to escaping from the institutional phase of the organizational life cycle.

9. He told an interviewer that his efforts were dominated by four messages:

Competitiveness —"be number one or a strong number two in your business or get out"

Realism—"don't finesse the numbers, tell it like it is, address the harsh realities of your situation"

Excellence—"we must be the best at what we do"

Entrepreneurship—"take a swing, take risks, we will not punish a well-reasoned and well-executed failure"

10. This has been the case with GM and EDS, and the former's CEO, Ross Perot, has made his frustration with the situation abundantly and publicly clear by his noisy departure from the GM board.

Chapter Six

1. See especially Sandra Krebs Hirsh, *Using the Myers-Briggs Type Indicator in Organizations: A Resource Book* (Palo Alto, CA: Consulting Psychologists Press, 1991, 1985) and *Introduction to Type in Organizational Settings* (Palo Alto, CA: Consulting Psychologists Press, 1987), which Hirsh wrote with Jean M. Kummerow. The more general books on type by Kiersey, Kroeger and Thuesen, and Myers (see Appendix B) are also useful.

2. See "Type and Occupation" in Isabel Briggs Myers, *Gifts Differing* (Palo Alto, CA: Consulting Psychologists Press, 1990, 1980), pp. 157–174.

3. For an extended discussion of the situational dimension of leadership, see "Leadership and Transition" in *Surviving Corporate Transition* (Mill Valley, CA: William Bridges & Associates, 1990), pp. 119–134.

4. Personifying an organization as I am doing in this book bothers some people—especially –NT–s and –ST–s, who see organizations much more mechanistically. What I mean by impatience is that the organization keeps trying to turn its attention toward the external and the logical and lacks good ways to compensate for this tendency. People who try to swim against this tide are overlooked, devalued, and blocked by all kinds of procedures and convention. What I am calling impatience is what it feels like to the affected individual, and it comes from the organization's characteristic style, which is built into the very structure and policy of the organization, not just the personal actions of a few key figures.

5. Remember that type designations mean only a preponderance of or tendency toward one end of the four polarities. Some extraverts, for example, have (or have developed) a high degree of introversion in their awareness and skills.

Index